LIVE LIFE IN W.O.W!

Nuggets
of Wonder, Openness
& Wisdom

Compiled by

Debora J. Hollick

Smash Through Mentor Ltd. Presents:

Live Life In W.O.W!

Nuggets of Wonder, Openness & Wisdom

Copyright © Debora J. Hollick 2022

First Edition 2022

ISBN: 978-1-7387899-0-0

Disclaimer

Any books, classes, programs, or material, presented by Debora J. Hollick and/or the Smash Through Mentor Ltd., are copyright. They are designed and intended for fun, growth, empowerment, informational, motivational, educational, and thought-provoking purposes only. They are sold or given with the understanding that the presenter, trainer, author, or publisher, is not engaged to render any type of psychological, legal, or any other kind of professional advice. The ideas, content or suggestions are the sole expression and opinion of its author. No warranties or guarantees are expressed or implied by the presenter or author. The presenter or author shall not be liable for any physical, psychological, emotional, mental, or damages of any sort whatsoever, including but not limited to special, incidental, consequential damages.

Our views and rights are such that everyone is responsible for their own choices, actions, and results.

DEDICATION

This book is dedicated to all of the authors who are brave enough to be vulnerable and open in sharing their stories and experiences, and the people who have encouraged them along the way.

Writing about personal experiences is not an easy thing to do. It is done with hope that by doing so, someone out there in this big, wide World, relates to what they say and their W.O.W! and will know they are not alone.

There is always hope.

FOREWORD

When Debora asked me to write the foreword to her book, I was honoured. I'm proud of her because when she came to me, she started with an idea and asked me if I thought it was a good one. I agreed and so she gathered fifteen amazing people to write their stories of W.O.W. - Wonder, Openness and Wisdom.

One of the first stories you'll read is about Olivia. Your first impression is that she's cute because she wears these funky heart-shaped glasses. But don't ever call her 'cute' because she'll tell you how sassy and savvy she is instead. And I use those words in a positive way. I loved her acronym for S.A.V.V.Y. and she teaches how you too can be S.A.V.V.Y. in business and life.

As your read Stuart's story about the camping trip in a Zimbabwe, Africa game reserve; you will learn how he applied his A.A.C. technique when he came face to face with an elephant, antelope, and a family of baboons. He even came across a family of warthogs; one of them even touched his leg. Yikes! Read his chapter to learn how he reacted.

I've often heard the expression, as one soul dies, another is born. Michelle shares a very heartfelt story of a client of hers who gave birth to a healthy baby boy while her mom, the grandmother, passed on. She received comfort in believing that perhaps her mom, the grandmother, met her grandson as he prepared to be born. Michelle is someone who walks between two worlds of birth and death.

Imagine being diagnosed with two different cancers just 39 days apart. What would I do? I have no clue. But Tammy does. You need to read Tammy's chapter of how she gets through cancer life with humour, positive mindset, and gratitude.

When I read Gina's chapter, she shared the work she does; counseling and helping management to recognize addiction in their businesses. Addiction affects the workplace in many ways. She knows this because she is a recovered addict herself. As she says in her chapter; nobody chooses to become an addict.

When you start reading Mila's chapter, you are instantly intrigued by the title of her chapter, Beat The B*tches. You will learn about the sneaky maneuvers she did at summer camp including getting caught by THE Jane Fonda while going late night skinny dipping. How fun that must have been. Hehehe.

Katy's chapter had me laughing my ass off when she got down on one knee and proposed to her resident client as she took off his support stockings. He was giggling in delight. Who does that? Katy does that. She loves teaching teams about laughter and how to get re-energized and reduce stress in the workplace.

In Ric's chapter you will learn about the devastating situation that caused him incredible financial loss and heartache, and how he bounced back. Amongst all the hardship he realized he still had a wonderful life with a beautiful, loving family. This situation made him evaluate his life and pursue his lifelong dream of being a photographer. Now he's been invited to submit to team Canada for the World Photographic Cup. It's like the Olympics for photographers!

I was very intrigued with LaDonna's title - God is a Very Funny Man. Sometimes I wonder why we should even consider making plans and setting goals when we might not know what God's plans are for us. LaDonna shares the story of her teenage daughter's pregnancy and the lessons they learned. Learn how funny God can be in LaDonna's chapter.

I really resonated with Lois' story because I am an artist myself. Her story of going to Alaska to embrace her spiritual gifts and being told to become a psychic artist, taught me that you are supposed to trust those whispers of your heart even when you don't totally understand what is going on. What does a psychic artist do? You'll learn all about it in Lois' chapter.

We often hear that laughter is the greatest medicine, but how about singing? Now mix in people with dementia. Can people with dementia learn to sing? In Amy's chapter we learn how singing + dementia = choir.

When you come to Toni's chapter, The Ring, you know it has something to do with a ring, but what else do you learn? I loved reading Toni's story because I have met her in person and she's such a beautiful soul. I heard the story of how her husband had a heart attack on a cruise, but I did not know anything else about him. Her chapter shares how the circle of a ring means forever. Forever loved. Forever now. The circle is never-ending.

Be a duck? What's that about? It certainly made me think. In Debora's chapter she shares when people make comments, they could hurt people's feelings. We need to be more considerate, caring and less judgmental. But if someone says something that hurts your feelings, you need to be a duck! Be a duck means, just let it slide off your back and swim away. Let it go and move on.

I always wondered if teddy bears were real and in Teresa's chapter you learn how she receives fur coats and makes them into teddy bears. There's so much more to this story! Read this chapter to learn about the teddy bears coming to life.

Overall, I learned so much from each person's story and that's what makes this book special. The stories. The people. The vulnerability they each share. They pour their hearts out in this book and it will keep you wondering about the wisdom and openness that each of these authors share.

Kelly Falardeau

TABLE OF CONTENTS

ACKNOWLEDGMENTS

Where and how does one begin?

My family, friends, and colleagues, you know who you are, thank you for your support. I appreciate and love you all.

I have been blessed to have many people in my life who have encouraged and believed in me, along my journey. Far too many to name without missing anyone.

That having been said, I would like to mention the following people, not because they are more important than anyone else, but because they have had a significant contribution to this achievement.

Is it customary or even proper protocol to thank someone who is no longer physically with us? I don't see why not, so I'm going to do it anyway,

Dr. Agnnes Kraweck *(yes, that is the correct spelling),* was one of my greatest mentors, supporters, and strongest, most enthusiastic encourager! She pioneered many things, spoke on many stages, TV, and Radio Shows, sharing her positivity, teaching Law of Attraction, and what Kirlian Photography can teach us about thought energy.

Not many were privileged to work with Agnnes, but I was one of the lucky few who did. I was also able to call her my friend. We spent many a lunch and dinner together, sharing thoughts, ideas, hopes and dreams, while she openly shared her knowledge with me.

She once told me I was going to greater things than she ever did, and she made me believe it! I'm not quite there yet, but I'm doing my best to prove her right.

Agnnes taught me so much and while I miss her very much, I know she is with me in Spirit, still guiding and inspiring me.

Another person who has had a considerably influential part in this book coming to fruition is **Corey Poirier**, bLU Talks founder, TEDx speaker, Author, Host of several Podcasts, including his most recent, The Enlightened Passenger.

Had he not reached out and encouraged me to participate in Vol 3 of the bLU Talks compilation series, I don't think I would have started writing and speaking, as much as I have during the last 2 to 3 years, if at all.

That invitation led me, through the bLU Talks community, to becoming a regular contributing writer to an online magazine called *Modern Warrior*. The Publisher, **Maria Rea**, seemed to enjoy my stories, which gave me more confidence to continue.

And then there is the fabulous **Kelly Falardeau**, who inspires me, and I'm sure many others, daily, in too many ways to count.

Kelly has also been a major source of me being able to believe that people really do need and want to hear what I have to say.

This was and still is sometimes, something I have struggled with for the vast majority of my life. More on this in another book I am writing titled, *The Bully Lives Within,* which I plan to publish during 2023.

I am honored that Kelly has graciously written the foreword to this book as well as participated as one of the co-authors. Her story is important and needs to be shared and I'm glad she chose to share it here.

One more person I would like to acknowledge is **Charmaine Hammond**, transformational speaker, radio host, and best-selling, award-winning author of five books, for graciously sharing her time and wisdom with me. Without her the *Live Life in W.O.W! Nuggets of Wonder, Openness & Wisdom Playbook*, likely wouldn't have happened. Having a companion book was her idea.

I love and appreciate you all.

Thank you!

INTRODUCTION
THE W.O.W! CONCEPT

This is the first book in a planned series of books and events.

It has been Divinely inspired and is more than an anthology book filled with life stories written by amazing authors, new and seasoned, shared to inspire and aspire those attracted to reading them.

It has been designed to help us all through these, and future, trying and even tumultuous times.

The timing of its release, along with all who choose to participate in its birth and growth, have been chosen by loving forces, guiding us along our way.

I am very proud of the authors who chose to share in this journey with me. I feel their stories are vulnerable, authentic, and powerful. They share their experiences openly, hoping that someone who may be feeling alone, embarrassed, or they themselves vulnerable, to their own situation or circumstances, will know that someone else has experienced or is experiencing, something similar.

The stories shared in this book range from being very serious, life and death, to practical and fun.

There is a story about camping and Hollywood movie stars and one about the jungles of Africa,

Another is all about bouncing back from financial devastation and betrayal.

There is also one about current issues involving addiction in the workplace, which is rampant in today's society. Is this something affecting you, someone you know or love?

And let's not forget the loveable teddy bears, and oh, so much more...

For those who choose to participate in living and sharing the concept of looking for the nuggets in all experiences, we believe it promises to be a future of learning and growth.

We hope you will share your W.O.W! nuggets with us, just as each author has done. Perhaps yours will be similar or altogether different. Regardless, we would love it if you wanted to begin create a dialogue with us.

We appreciate and thank you for purchasing *LIVE LIFE IN W.O.W! Nuggets of Wonder, Openness & Wisdom* and the companion *Playbook*, for yourself and others. There is a reason you are here, right now, being drawn to it. It will be as individual as each of us.

The intention is, for this concept to become a movement.

Will you join us in future books in the series or by becoming involved in or attending events that we plan to be associated with it?

I hope so.

LET'S MAKE IT HAPPEN, TOGETHER!

W.O.W! SUMMARIES

OLIVIA VO

As the author of this chapter, in the living of this experience and in the writing of it to share with you, my readers, I would like to summarize my W.O.W! Nuggets. I see them as the:

WONDER - Communication gaps and generational gaps are vibrational. We see a rise in immigrant families or displaced people who are vibrating at one level for survival. Parents who are doing the best they can with what they have and know in order to work hard, save money, and make sure their kids survive too.

OPENNESS - Being able to forgive my parents for any misunderstanding and no matter what, I can make myself proud. For them coming to America was about survival and they didn't see it as a dream at that time. As an adult, I saw returning to my birthplace of Vietnam as the dream and that is a much different vibration of excitement than fear.

WISDOM - The heart-shaped glasses found their way to me! They represent my highest vibration for positivity and kindness. When I wear my heart glasses, I am sending an awesome uplifting vibration out to those around me.

I invite you to contact me and Debora J. Hollick, the author of this book, to let us know if you feel the same as I did or if not, to please share your W.O.W! Nuggets with us at:

Contact Olivia:
oliviavo.savvysocialpro@gmail.com

Contact Debora:
https://www.linkedin.com/in/deborajhollick/

STUART ELLIOTT

As the author of this chapter, in the living of this experience and in the writing of it to share with you, my readers, I would like to summarize my W.O.W! Nuggets. I see them as the:

WONDER - I am in awe of all the wonderful possibilities that exist when me make choices consciously rather than simply react to situations.

OPENNESS - Accepting that I did not always realize I was acting from automaticity rather than conscious choice, and this was limiting my happiness.

WISDOM - No matter what happens to us in life, we always have the choice of how we react to it and that gives us the power to control our happiness.

I invite you to contact me and Debora J. Hollick, the author of this book, to let us know if you feel the same as I did or if not, to please share your W.O.W! Nuggets with us at:

Contact Stuart:
https://my.link.gallery/stuart

Contact Debora:
https://www.linkedin.com/in/deborajhollick/

MICHELLE SMITH

As the author of this chapter, in the living of this experience and in the writing of it to share with you, my readers, I would like to summarize my W.O.W! Nuggets. I see them as the:

WONDER - There is nothing like being present for labor and birth. To witness a woman's strength, baby's first breath and their first cry, and then the tears, joy and wonder of the parents and family present is beyond description. There is also wonder in watching someone take their last breath as their life force leaves their body. These are sacred moments in life that not everyone has the honor to hold space for. Perhaps if we did and these moments were always treated as the holy events they are, our world might be a more loving and compassionate place.

OPENNESS - Being present during pregnancy and birth, as well as in death, grief, and loss, has taught me to be open and non-judgmental. I have found that healing occurs when there is a compassionate presence who allows someone to feel held in their raw and vulnerable moments, and that their experience is seen, heard, and validated.

WISDOM - The secret is in surrender. To be in control in labor requires surrendering to the process of birth. There is a surrender required when we die. We also must surrender to the reality that someone we love is dying. Birth, breath, death, and grief have taught me to surrender my need to control things and trust in the wisdom of forces greater than myself.

I invite you to contact me and Debora J. Hollick, the author of this book, to let us know if you feel the same as I did or if not, to please share your W.O.W! Nuggets with us at:

Contact Michelle:
Michelle@birtheaseservices.com

Contact Debora:
https://www.linkedin.com/in/deborajhollick/

TAMMY RADER

As the author of this chapter, in the living of this experience and in the writing of it to share with you, my readers, I would like to summarize my W.O.W! Nuggets. I see them as the:

WONDER - I amazed myself that I had the strength, courage and resilience to come through like a champion! I didn't realize I was this stubborn.

OPENNESS - It's opened doors for me that I never thought of before, like becoming a #1 International Best Selling Author! It opened me up to living in the **HERE** and **NOW**, not in the past or the future.

WISDOM - Is in the BE-ing. Here is a great quote from Les Brown: "The graveyard is the richest place on earth, because it is here that you will find all the hopes and dreams that were never fulfilled, the books that were never written, the songs that were never sung, the inventions that were never shared, the cures that were never discovered, all because someone was too afraid to take that first step, keep with the problem, or determined to carry out their dream."

I invite you to contact me and Debora J. Hollick, the author of this book, to let us know if you feel the same as I did or if not, to please share your W.O.W! Nuggets with us at:

Contact Tammy:
Email: Tammy@beyoutiful.health
LinkedIn: linkedin.com/in/tammyrader

Contact Debora:
https://www.linkedin.com/in/deborajhollick/

GINA CATHERINE VANDERHAM, M.A.

As the author of this chapter, in the living of this experience and in the writing of it to share with you, my readers, I would like to summarize my W.O.W! Nuggets. I see them as the:

WONDER - Is evidence of God moving in my life to restore me to health, and the real fact that one can recover from life-threatening addiction with the help of a loving God.

OPENNESS - My experience of getting sober and getting into recovery opened me up to Faith being alive within me and it brought me back from the brink of death. I went from the walking dead to be more fully aware, alive, and present in my life, free of addiction and recovering one day at a time.

WISDOM – No one ever wakes up and says, "Gee, I'd like to be an addict." There should be no shame in addiction, nor should people be shamed or judged. The concern should be what happened to you (compassion), not what's wrong with you (judgement/shaming).

Addiction in the workplace is rampant. Help your workplace be a significant contributing factor in an employee's or colleague's recovery. You may be saving a life.

I invite you to contact me and Debora J. Hollick, the author of this book, to let us know if you feel the same as I did and if not, to please share your W.O.W! Nuggets with us at:

Contact Gina:
https://www.linkedin.com/in/gina-vanderham-ma-mft-icadc-sap-rcc-phsa-b544051/
ginavanderham@gmail.com
www.ginavanderham.com

Contact Debora:
https://www.linkedin.com/in/deborajhollick/

MILA JOHANSEN

As the author of this chapter, in the living of this experience and in the writing of it to share with you, my readers, I would like to summarize my W.O.W! Nuggets. I see them as the:

WONDER - It's amazing when we find our voice and speak out. It makes us appreciate all who came before us speaking against injustices and other travesties. We all have a voice to speak out and inspire.

OPENNESS - Being open to learning and open to new ideas leads us down the road to our future. The power of saying YES can open doors we never knew existed. Saying YES, whenever we can presents us with all the wondrous possibilities.

WISDOM - One step at a time—but keep stepping forward. It seems the more I give freely as often as I can, it creates unlimited abundance for me. It's like a puzzle. I try to give in all sorts of ways without being caught and I have so much fun doing it.

Do all the good you can, by all the means you can, in all the ways you can, in all the places you can, at all the times you can, to all the people you can, as long as ever you can. ~John Wesley

I invite you to contact me and Debora J. Hollick, the author of this book, to let us know if my story resonated with you or not and to share your W.O.W.! Nuggets with us.

Contact Mila:
milajohansen.com johansenmila@gmail.com
https://www.linkedin.com/in/mila-johansen-pentopublished/

Contact Debora:
https://www.linkedin.com/in/deborajhollick/

KATY MAAG

As the author of this chapter, in the living of this experience and in the writing of it to share with you, my readers, I would like to summarize my W.O.W! Nuggets. I see them as the:

WONDER - is how I could allow someone to say something so untrue and to believe what he or she said without questioning let alone to believe. That would be their opinion.

OPENNESS - The openness that I had was that I needed to stand up and have the confidence.

WISDOM - It really was a blessing that I sought help to sort through my past and deal with the present. I learned to stand up for myself and do what gives me pleasure, like having enough confidence to share my story and facilities stress management and laughter for others wellness.

I invite you to contact me and Debora J. Hollick, the author of this book, to let us know if you feel the same as I did and if not, to please share your W.O.W! Nuggets with us at:

Contact Katy:
Website: KMwellnessconsulting.com
Email: 1katymaag@gmail.com

Contact Debora:
https://www.linkedin.com/in/deborajhollick/

KELLY FALARDEAU

As the author of this chapter, in the living of this experience and in the writing of it to share with you, my readers, I would like to summarize my W.O.W! Nuggets. I see them as the:

WONDER - Instead of wondering what would have happened if I hadn't become a coach and just stayed stuck on the couch; I wonder what else can I do to help people in the author world? I wonder what else I can teach my clients so they can take their stories and careers to a whole new level. One thing I love about the internet, there's so many incredible opportunities. We have to say to ourselves "What else can I do?" And when you do that, you open up your mind to the 'wonder' and mystery of the world.

When you ask that question, your brain says, "Hmm, I wonder, what else can we do?" Ask your brain a question and it wants to solve it. Tell yourself a statement "I can't do that!" And your brain says, "You're right, you can't."

OPENNESS - These past two years have allowed me to open myself to even more opportunities than ever before. I've learned to accept that I am a coach. People want to learn my system and strategies, and I am worth charging higher fees so my clients can become bestselling authors and take their businesses to the next level.

I am a coach and it's time to embrace it and keep supporting people in their book writing journey.

WISDOM - Is that change is not all bad. Yes, change can be difficult and scary at times. We get scared because of the fear of the unknown, but we need to learn how to embrace fear and change. Had I not embraced coaching people to write their books and become bestselling authors, I may have become broke and broken. Instead, I found a way to create another revenue source for my business and support my kids financially in a way I couldn't before. Plus, I help my clients create an impact and income which gives me immense satisfaction.

I invite you to contact me and Debora J. Hollick, the author of this book, to let us know if you feel the same as I did and if not, to please share your W.O.W! Nuggets with us at:

Contact Kelly:
https://linktr.ee/kellynft

Contact Debora:
https://www.linkedin.com/in/deborajhollick/

RIC MATKOWSKI

As the author of this chapter, in the living of this experience and in the writing of it to share with you, my readers, I would like to summarize my W.O.W! Nuggets. I see them as the:

WONDER: Abundance exists all around us, there are no limitations. None!

OPENNESS: The Universe is ready to deliver, be deserving and you will receive. Focus on the positive and when you drift, just change the story running in your head. Refocus and run more supportive stories.

WISDOM: Life is life. Things happen but the magic is in not dwelling upon those negatives, but to move on, forgive yourself, and live in the moment. We cannot change the past, nor should we dwell on the future, because anything we think might happen is not truth. It is a story we've made up of something that has not happened! Live today. Be the person that does the things that will let you have all that you want. And...live in constant gratitude.

I invite you to contact me and Debora J. Hollick, the author of this book, to let us know if my story resonated with you or not and to share your W.O.W.! Nuggets with us at:

Contact Ric:
Website: https://www.imagesbyric.com

Contact Debora:
https://www.linkedin.com/in/deborajhollick/

LADONNA MCABEE

As the author of this chapter, in the living of this experience and in the writing of it to share with you, my readers, I would like to summarize my W.O.W! Nuggets. I see them as the:

WONDER – I didn't know how much I needed Seth to come into my and my family's life or how much we would all learn about patience, compassion, and love, through one amazing child.

OPENNESS – I opened up to turning negatives into positives as much as possible, and learning to react in loving and helpful ways, or to not respond at all. Keep an open mind and show love regardless of what the situation may be.

WISDOM - It's not always about you or the person talking. Your reaction needs to be loving and helpful or not respond at all. Our Plan is not always what God has planned for us. Remember that a challenge is a situation that you are in control of making decisions or consequences.
Help others with loving choices so they can make their decisions with a open mind and heart. Don't judge and try to make decisions for them.

I invite you to contact me and Debora J. Hollick, the author of this book, to let us know if you feel the same as I did and if not, to please share your W.O.W! Nuggets with us at:

Contact LaDonna:
www.homesweethometreasures.net
Facebook.com/HomeSweetHomeTreasures1

Contact Debora:
https://www.linkedin.com/in/deborajhollick/

LOIS WARNOCK

As the author of this chapter, in the living of this experience and in the writing of it to share with you, my readers, I would like to summarize my W.O.W! Nuggets. I see them as the:

WONDER - The amazing opportunities we have when we connect to the spirit realm along with the 'Divine/Universe/God'. I live my days excited to see what spirit leads me to, and how I can share and be of service to humanity.

OPENNESS - I AM open to the Divine, I AM unique, I AM curious, I AM open to the infinite possibilities to grow and manifest the life I dream about!

WISDOM - The more I learn, the more I realize what I don't know! The wisdom I have gained through all my experiences cannot be measured. Every experience you have 'good or not' can be a learning step to help you and others. Your wisdom awaits someone else needing a miraculous message!

I invite you to contact me and Debora J. Hollick, the author of the book, to let us know if you feel the same as I did or if not, to please share your W.O.W! Nuggets with us at:

Contact Lois
https://linktr.ee/loiswarnock

Contact Debora:
https://www.linkedin.com/in/deborajhollick/

AMY STANDRIDGE

As the author of this chapter, in the living of this experience and in the writing of it to share with you, my readers, I would like to summarize my W.O.W! Nuggets. I see them as the:

WONDER - I experience a sense of wonder when families welcome me into their hearts and share their lives with me. I think relationships are a wonder.

OPENNESS - I want others to have an openness to try a new artistic skill or activity or revisit an old skill or hobby they may have neglected for far too long.

WISDOM - I believe that it is wise to continue to reach out to the offerings of your community if you or your loved one ever receives a negative diagnosis. There is still beauty and joy. Sometimes you need others to help you find it.

I invite you to contact me and Debora J. Hollick, the author of this book, to let us know if you

feel the same as I did or if not, to please share your W.O.W! Nuggets with us at:

Contact Amy:
amy@oaksongmusictherapy.com
https://www.linkedin.com/in/amy-standridge/
https://www.facebook.com/oaksongmt
https://www.youtube.com/amystandridge

Contact Debora:
https://www.linkedin.com/in/deborajhollick/

TONI KAUFMAN

As the author of this chapter, in the living of this experience and in the writing of it to share with you, my readers, I would like to summarize my W.O.W! Nuggets. I see them as the:

WONDER: Sharing my life with a wonderful man, who was flawed, and was real, the connection after all is said and done, comes back around to marrying your best friend.

OPENNESS: Getting married is easy, **STAYING** married is a lot of work! Without shame and in the spirit of complete openness, I share what was my life was like for the 33 years of my marriage.

WISDOM: It's ok to love someone with all their faults, trials and experiences that come with it. All of us are imperfect beings and works in progress. However, it doesn't mean we can't set boundaries that can be mutually beneficial.

I invite you to contact me and Debora J. Hollick, the author of this book, to let us know if you feel the same as I did and if not, to please share your W.O.W! Nuggets with us at:

Contact Toni:
https://linktr.ee/tonikaufman

Contact Debora:
https://www.linkedin.com/in/deborajhollick/

DEBORA J. HOLLICK

As the author of this chapter, in the living of this experience and in the writing of it to share with you, my readers, I would like to summarize my W.O.W! Nuggets. I see them as the:

WONDER – Is how much better I feel when I look for good in others and that I can always find something.

OPENNESS – I've opened up to trying to be less sensitive about what others say and do.

WISDOM – Give the benefit of the doubt, lessen your own burdens by not casting judgement so quickly. Let the minor things flow off your back, like a duck allows the water.

I invite you to contact me, Debora J. Hollick, the author of this book, to let me know if you feel the same as I did and if not, to please share your W.O.W! Nuggets with me at:

Contact Debora:
https://www.linkedin.com/in/deborajhollick/
Debora@smashthroughmentor.com

TERESA BRUNNER

As the author of this chapter, in the living of this experience and in the writing of it to share with you, my readers, I would like to summarize my W.O.W! Nuggets. For me, my:

WONDER - To me they were just my teddy bear stories. Who would want to know more about them other than the people whom I made the teddy bears for? In fact, the wonder is, that I have excited many others with my stories and now they realize the importance of creating a legacy for their family.

OPENNESS - Sharing some of my stories has helped me realize that I am helping loved ones create a legacy from their fur coats that hold so much love, are valued and hold great importance for those who wore them. It is both a privilege and honor to be a part of that journey.

WISDOM - It's not about the teddy bears, it's about the stories they tell, how they make you feel, and how you remember the person who gave you the teddy bear. This includes, the person wearing the coat, what you were doing with the person when they wore the coat, touching and feeling the fur and most of all, the love you feel in your heart when you hug your teddy bear.

I invite you to contact me and Debora J. Hollick, the author of this book, to let us know if you feel the same as I did or if not, to please share your W.O.W! Nuggets with us at:

Contact Teresa:
Website: www.teddymybear.com
Email: teddymybearteresa@gmail.com

Contact Debora:
https://www.linkedin.com/in/deborajhollick/

Olivia Vo is a heart-centered entrepreneur and founder of Savvy Social Enterprises, where she infuses her joyful energy, humor style, and savvy strategies for online collaborations and livestreaming productions.

Her S.A.V.V.Y. list includes her teaching skills, positive attitude as her best attribute, collaboration as her value, victorious about being a digital entrepreneur, and creating diamond art to keep her young-at-heart.

She credits the LinkedIn platform with providing her very first career in staffing as a recruiter and now as her livelihood as a social media content creator.

She is a member of AATH (Association for Applied Therapeutic Humor) organization and is currently enrolled in a three-year program with The Humor Academy to earn her Humor Professional Certification.

In addition, she is trained in Laughter Yoga, and her certification is recognized by Dr. Madan Kataria of Laughter Yoga International University India. Olivia has also received the 200-hour Yoga Teacher Training from Yoga Den Mandarin in Jacksonville, Florida.

Olivia is available to speak on the health benefits of laughter yoga for your organization or event, and leads fun, engaging workshops and laughter exercises, easily applicable for your own self-care.

Olivia facilitates hands-on trainings and workshops both for in-person and online virtual events.

She is known for her ability to connect and energize groups through her infectious laughter, empathy, and winsome smile.

She has worked with thousands of people of all ages and all abilities to boost their best and to relieve intense stress.

Follow Olivia at #SavvySocialCollab and #SavvySocialSaturday on LinkedIn.

www.linkedin.com/in/oliviavo-savvysocialpro

HOW DID THESE HEART-SHAPED GLASSES FIND ME?
BY OLIVIA VO

I've always followed my heart and pursued my dreams, and I imagine that people find that inspiring. I hope that is the effect I have on my fans and people in general. I definitely want to project a positive energy out into the world. ~ Britney Spears

"Adorable."

"Cute."

"Cutie."

"Fun."

"Charming."

Whenever someone describes me in this manner in the office or business setting, I feel rather uncomfortable and uneasy, especially since I am a new entrepreneur, looking to "make it." I want to be taken seriously. I don't want to be known for "cute" or that my ideas are "cute" and therefore can never take off or be truly considered.

Recently, I was asked, by a business colleague, "What's your story behind your heart glasses?" I smiled and shared how they found and chose me. It went something like this:

On weekends, I volunteer for a local nonprofit called Harmony Mind Body Spirit Wellness, and I host a variety of playful, laughter exercises and activities for kids at the Jacksonville Arboretum and Botanical Gardens. As such I am constantly searching for fun props, toys, and games to engage the children.

I recall one particular week before Valentine's Day. I'm in Walmart, browsing its aisles for holiday décor and shopping for fun greeting cards for the kids to exchange with one another. I gathered plenty of conversation heart candies, stickers, puzzles, and then, looming large on the shelf was an organized display of boxes with a sign in bright, bold letters, **"Valentine, I think you're Spec-tacular!"** Each of these boxes contained heart-shaped glasses! The clever sign and play on words referred to spec as in spectacles. I quickly picked up several boxes and threw them into my shopping cart. I loved these glasses, and they were the perfect kid-size, and I was sure the kids would be delighted too.

As I rounded the corner of the aisle, there was another display of adult heart-shaped lens less glasses! They had a unique almost vintage cat eye shape to them with exaggerated heart frames and vibrant red color. I burst out laughing as I admired myself in the mirror trying on the glasses. They were an exact fit.

Needless to say, I wore my glasses to the park and the kids really gravitated towards me and my new look. They also enjoyed exchanging the *spec-tacular* Valentine greeting cards and wearing their colorful heart spectacles too.

It was just way too much fun for all of us!

Creating a strong self-image, online persona, and brand is integral to being recognized in business. I have spent the first year of my business identifying who I am and what I represent. Although I embrace my exuberant, joyful countenance and positivity, I long to be seen for more than that.

After cultivating a staffing and recruiting career for a decade, my first foray into entrepreneurship was conducting LinkedIn social media training and helping people update their profiles. I was "given" titles such as Trainer, Specialist, and Authority and although I tried them on in earnest, they still did not suit me. It was as if I were trying on shoes that were too small and tight, making my toes feel crammed. I felt uncomfortable and kept tripping and teetering on my feet.

Running parallel to formulating my LinkedIn business, I received training in Laughter Yoga. I was able to discover a community of laughter yogis through my extensive online networking. With my Laughter Yoga training, I appreciate my inner child and being able to adopt childlike play and wonder. It is a blessing to know that I can be simply who I am and express myself in genuine, creative ways, and encourage others to connect to their young-at-heart selves too.

BRANDING WITH STYLE

One day during a Zoom meeting with my Lunch and Learn Zoom Fridays group, I wore my heart glasses just for fun. I was surprised by how many compliments came through the chat and that people really liked them on me. A close colleague, Helen Snell, said that I "had the sort of face that the glasses just go with it" and that, "I could pull it off."

I began to wear them exclusively for all my virtual meetings and from there the glasses just *stuck*. I am grateful for the glasses since they are an excellent icebreaker and conversation piece. People instantly recognized me for them, and it has become my signature look and has morphed into its own brand. By wearing the glasses, I have also become bolder stepping into the spotlight.

For most of my recruiting career, I focused on playing by the rules, and going by the book. In entrepreneurship, I love the freedom of choice and that I get to make my own decisions and make my own rules.

Regarding the Lunch and Learn Zoom Fridays group, we call ourselves heart-centered entrepreneurs, and here I am really embodying it.

I now have an array of fabulous glasses, in almost every color, to not only coordinate with my outfits, but my mood, too.

Have you ever heard the expression about people who *wear their heart on their sleeves?* It indicates they show their emotions very openly. I've adopted my own mantra in that I wear my heart on my face because through my heart-shaped glasses, I see everything with loving eyes. I do my best to find the love – the good – in everyone and everything. This mantra has served me well when faced with disappointments and discord.

Clients who have collaborated with me always share that they enjoy being in my presence. They can see how much I care and how invested I am in their personal success. The fact that the hearts are so exaggerated and magnified speaks to how big my own heart is and in how I show kindness. One of the best comments I've received came from a LinkedIn connection, Marty Morgan, "Olivia, you have a way of leaving people better than you found them."

The heart-shaped glasses have also become a wonderful visual asset, since part of my business is video livestreaming, creating video podcasts, virtual events, and promotions. The glasses are eye-catching, noticeable, and contribute to me having a "big personality" that helps attract viewers and further boosts my brand recognition and success.

Recently, I attended a conference for the United States Women Entrepreneurship Cooperative. For five months, I was part of a cohort of entrepreneurial women. We gathered online for classes, meetings, and business assignments. When we finally met in-person, so many of my colleagues sought me out and commented how they already felt as if they "knew" me just because of my glasses, and that I had stepped out of the Zoom video to appear in real life.

Had I attended the conference without the glasses, I suspect they would not have recognized me as readily. The glasses have made me into a celebrity! I do admit that there are times when I feel the glasses are my digital, virtual self and I need to reconcile that with my analog self, too. I often get asked, "Do the glasses ever come off?" Yes, when I'm at home with my spouse or close friends, I don't wear them and take them off when I'm out and about in public. I hope that with or without glasses, people would come to know me just as well and that my essence remains the same.

SAVVY SOCIAL STRATEGIST - REVEALED

Finally, with my visual identity and business model intact, I needed to address that there was still the missing moniker. It was time to brainstorm again with my Lunch and Learn Zoom Fridays group.

Here's what I knew so far – I am a natural social butterfly. I love to socialize. I enjoy learning and teaching social media, gaining visibility for clients on platforms like LinkedIn and Restream. Another colleague remarked how much they liked my step-by-step guidance and instructions, methodology, and strategic approach. They saw me as a Strategist. So, we came up with Social Strategist. We knew there had to be another "S" word to make this complete. I'm known for my stylish outfits, and I have a sleek, short, bob haircut, then that's when the word "savvy" came to mind!

That is how **Savvy Social Strategist** came to be...and the shoes fit! The heart-shaped glasses authentically helped to seal in that composite self-image. It clicks for people, too, when I introduce myself as **Olivia Vo, Savvy Social Pro**. They see it right away...and it is so far, far, away from cute!

Savvy truly speaks to my creativity and there's a certain way that I do things, especially when I teach, train, share tips, and make adult learning interesting, engaging, and memorable.

Over time I have developed a special acronym for the word **S.A.V.V.Y**.

I invite you to consider what makes you savvy! Come up with your own Savvy list of 25 things about you. For each letter, write out 5 items.

S: Skills or Services

What are your 5 unique skills, subject matter expertise, services you provide or perhaps speaking topics?

A: Attributes

What are 5 things you like about yourself?

V: Values

What are your top 5 causes that you support, or what do you stand for that's important to you?

V: Victories

What are 5 achievements or milestones you love to celebrate?

Y: Young-at-Heart

What are 5 hobbies, favorite activities, or things you like to do for fun and give you

youthful energy?

These types of lists are called listicles. I love this word! I suggest you allow these types of lists to be a powerful, quick reference guide for you when you're feeling "blah" and need a pick-me-up.

We need to be our own best encourager. Use this S.A.V.V.Y. list to remind yourself of how amazing, wonderful, and radiant you are!

I have incorporated this S.A.V.V.Y. concept into almost every client conversation. Moreover, it makes an excellent framework when you're planning your social media content.

To take the S.A.V.V.Y. method further, consider playing your favorite song or hyped-up music. Wrap yourself in a hug as you sway side to side and say "mmm hmmm," as if you were having a delicious bite of your favorite food! Recite your S.A.V.V.Y. list out loud with much feeling! Be intriguing, enticing, beguiling, and alluring.

This is a technique that has worked for many clients before they go on stage for a speaking engagement or before hitting that record button to go live. It helps put them in a positive frame of mind.

You can also follow #SavvySocialSaturday posts on LinkedIn and share your S.A.V.V.Y. list. These posts are designed to introduce you to social networking and boost your connections and followers. I enjoy spotlighting one person a week and talking about what makes them savvy as well as create a #SavvyMatch for referrals.

STAND UP – SHOW UP

As I write and reflect on this business branding experience, I have learned to stand up for myself.

No, I'm not cute.

I'd much rather you see me as savvy, and I can show you what makes you savvy too.

I think about the last major time that I had to stand up for myself. It was in my twenties and coming face-to-face with my parents.

This year I have been writing more than ever. Creative writing, storytelling, writing to teach and impart lessons or messages. Doing so has really opened up a new wonder in me that, I get to document and share some of my entrepreneurial journey and wisdom nuggets with others.

When asked, "What do you want to be when you grow up?" I recall telling my parents, very enthusiastically, "I want to be writer." They laughed. I believe their reaction was because they didn't see or understand that writing could be a worthwhile and serious profession.

I was 10 years old at the time and their reaction set me in a different life direction for quite a while.

Despite their teasing of me, I always kept writing in mind. I didn't give up and pursued writing in different ways. I excelled in my English Literature and AP English classes, got involved with poetry and my school's literary journal, research papers, and eventually was very adept at writing college essays for scholarship money. All those efforts eventually led to a US Fulbright Award.

Writing has brought me so many opportunities and the Fulbright was a crowning, glorious achievement, in which I could travel to my birth country of Vietnam and pursue volunteer work with the Peace Village Orphanage for children, affected by Agent Orange. Wow, I felt my writing really paid off!

I thought, in that moment, my parents would be proud of me, too, and see how writing helped me to develop and grow as a person. Their reaction of disappointment took me by surprise.

As a first-generation, college graduate from an immigrant family, they had pinned all their high hopes and ambitions for me to pursue loftier goals and complete grad school, to earn a doctorate and enter law or medicine. Why couldn't they be open to me forging my own individual path? All that they had sacrificed for me to have a proper education in America to where they escaped Vietnam from, did pay off and yet, they felt that it wasn't enough.

They almost forbade me to go, and I felt devastated that I was going to have to give up my dreams and Fulbright Award. In that moment, I found clarity of voice and reason, and stated to them, "Whether you approve or not, I am going to do it anyway."

Looking back, I recognize now how fearful they were of me going back to a country they had fled and all the associated painful memories it held for them. They took a risk and escaped communist rule of Vietnam, and here I was, with my suitcases packed, ready to go back to explore and better understand my heritage roots.

Growing up I witnessed my parents transform our family of five in a strange, unknown land. They taught me immeasurable values of hard work, persistence, bravery, tenacity, resilience in the midst of adversity, and to strive for opportunity. How was this any different, me venturing to Vietnam on those same principles of risk and courage?

This entire time, I was only following their example, doing exactly what they taught me during my school years and early career path. I was them and more, as I embarked on my Fulbright adventure, and now as I continue on with my entrepreneurial journey.

I loved and respected my parents (and still do, very much), but it was high time they got to see me for who I am, and it took my standing up to them and declaring what I wanted for my life.

They have achieved their version of the American Dream by putting their kids through college, buying, and owning their own home, and now it's time for me to claim my American Dream of entrepreneurship and operate a thriving savvy business and creating generational wealth.

I will make them, myself, and all others who are extremely vital in my entrepreneurial journey, proud indeed.

Stuart Elliott is known for helping people break free from the mental prison of negative self-talk that keeps them drained of passion and dissatisfied with life.

Through Mindful Hypnotic Life-Coaching he helps them snap out of their trance of unworthiness as they blast away whatever is holding them back. This frees them from the paralyzing uncertainty of how to connect to their passions and create a deeply fulfilling, happy life.

He was born in the UK and moved to Africa where he stayed for 18 years, then moved to the South of China where he currently resides.

Living for extended periods on these diverse continents has taught hm a lot about people and mindset in general. He's coupled this experience with the study of Conversational Hypnosis, NLP, Mindfulness and Positive Psychology to develop a system that helps you connect to fulfilling happiness.

When you have the right mindset, there is always a way to resolve any challenges you may face in your life.

And that's where his greatest pleasure lies. It's in helping you make the mindset shifts necessary to grow in happiness and life satisfaction.

He states: *"There is no other reward like seeing the smile that develops upon another person's face when they suddenly see the light."*

He truly believes that the time is ripe for you to shine and find your Garden of Eden.

If you'd like to find out more about how you can do that please visit:

https://my.link.gallery/stuart

THE ASTONISHING POWER OF CHOICE
BY STUART ELLIOTT

Success is something you attract through the person you become. ~ JIM ROHN

Let me ask you a question:

Who is it that makes YOU happy?

Is it a close friend, a family member, a pet or perhaps some external thing?

Take a moment to think about this...

You see by experiencing any or all of the above you can feel happier...and yet, by the same token, you can also allow these same things to trigger feelings of discomfort or anger in yourself.

Maybe the family member you're with just said something that riled you, or your pet just made a mess on the carpet, and you became angry because you'd recently been outside together.

Whatever it is, the incident then sets up an automatic reaction that triggers your emotions and takes away your control of the situation.

HOW I FELL FOR THE 'RAP TRAP'

Here's a good example of this type of incident in action.

A few years ago, I attended the 'leaving party' of a teaching colleague. He had booked a small bar for the party, and it was quite packed.

As I entered the bar I heard the jarring sounds of Rap Music playing loudly over the speakers. As the night wore on everyone in attendance was having a good time grooving to the music as they chatted with friends.

Except me...

To say I don't particularly like rap music is an understatement. I allowed the same rhythms that everybody else was enjoying triggering anger in me. I made what should have been a nice celebration and happy send off into a miserable night for myself because I didn't realize I had made the unconscious choice to react this way.

I was just triggered by the sounds and reacted negatively.

It never even occurred to me that I had the choice to allow myself to be bothered by the music or not, or even that I could choose to connect to the positive energy everyone else was sending out. I simply, unconsciously, chose the first option which allowed my emotions to get the better of me.

You see, it's not the incident or person that makes you happy. It's the way you **CHOOSE** to react to it that is the key to your happiness.

But how do you make that choice?

Well, that's the million-dollar question isn't it? So often we are triggered by events and then our emotions take over. Once they do, we forget we have choice, just like I did in the above tale.

And that's where the little understood power of...

A.A.C. COMES TO THE RESCUE

Where:

- **A = Awareness** of what is happening (an external event is triggering an emotion or similar)
- **A = Acceptance** that it is happening (time to step back for a moment and breathe deeply)

- **C = Choice** - This is a biggie. Understanding that we always have the choice of how we react to any situation is key

The principles of A.A.C. are deceptively simple and yet these three tenets of human nature are fundamental to our underlying well-being and personal happiness. For this reason, I think they demand to be taught at school.

After all, we are taught how to use 'A,B,C...' at a young age but we are never taught about 'A.A.C.' at all and yet this is a basic language of behavior. One that can have a greater impact on our overall well-being and happiness than ABC ever can.

When you use **Awareness, Acceptance and Choice** wisely every day of your life you are able to take charge of your happiness and contentment in ways you never thought possible.

Let's go over them in a little more detail, then I'll give you a real-life example of how I used them in a supremely powerful way.

It was so beautiful; I was left speechless for many minutes. W.O.W. cannot do justice to the way I felt. I was awestruck and just thinking about it again gives me goosebumps.

Awareness

From experience, I see many people only apply the understanding of awareness to external events. They know whether it is light or dark, rainy, or sunny or what time it is etc. Seldom are they aware of how they are reacting to things that happen in the moment, though.

Nevertheless, this is where we would be wise to focus a lot more of our attention. Being aware of what is going on inside our mind and body is key.

For instance, you might be talking with someone and suddenly notice that you've moved back fractionally. You become aware you are taking in a deep breath as you prepare to answer back in defiance. Once you notice that, you empower yourself to choose to take a more reasoned approach that might not end up in an argument or worse.

Thing is though, the trigger often happens so quickly that it can take us by surprise.

Road rage is a good example of this.

The path from incident to reaction is so rapid that we barely have time to notice how we've been triggered. Nonetheless, even amid the lightning speed of what is happening, we can learn to become aware of how we are reacting.

Once we do, we can quickly move into the next phase of A.A.C. which is Acceptance.

Acceptance

This is the metaphorical moment to breathe. It is your time to say to yourself: *"Oh, this event is making me react in an automatic way. Let me take a short moment to breathe and see how I want to respond to what has happened."*

Now that you have given yourself that moment of tranquility in the storm, you are freed to proceed from a place of personal power rather than get fired up by a string of emotions.

Please note that 'Acceptance' does not mean to accept the intent of the event, it is merely the action of noticing what is happening and accepting that it is happening. Thus, you give yourself the time to react in an intentional way rather than an 'out of control' way.

And that brings us to the 'juicy' part of A.A.C. - Choice.

Choice

Choice is interesting because many people feel powerless when confronted by events. They think they have no choice.

What they don't realize, however, is that by thinking that way they are in fact making a choice.

You see, no matter what happens in life, the reality is that we always have the power to choose how we react to the event. We may not have control over the event itself, but we can always choose how we react to it.

Granted, this may not be easy but, with practice, and the application of 'Awareness' and 'Acceptance' we get better and better about making choices. We are then able to take action from a place of understanding and power, rather than from the automatic choices borne from reaction or emotion.

And it does not matter how far down the 'automatic reaction road' you are. Once you decide to become aware of what is happening, and accept it, then you give yourself the power to choose how you want to proceed.

Here's that real-life story I promised you. It illustrates just how powerful the concepts of A.A.C. are when they are applied.

At One In The Bush

A few years ago, I was on a camping trip through the game reserves of Western Zimbabwe with a good friend of mine, Roy.

One night we decided to rent a small chalet in the Victoria Falls National Park. The chalet was on the banks of the Zambezi River not far upstream from the mighty, thundering Victoria Falls themselves.

As sunset was approaching, we decided to have a Braai (that's the local word for barbecue). I elected to build the fire whilst Roy prepared the meat.

The Braai area was about 30 feet from the house not far from some thick brush and trees. I duly gathered some choice wood and built it into a nice stack on top of the fireplace. It would be easy to light and quickly burn down to some satisfying coals.

As I was about to set a flame to the wood, I happened to glance up into the thick bush a few feet away and noticed there was an elephant standing there, casually watching me. It felt as though he was giving me the Zulu greeting of "I see you my friend."

Elephants are magnificent creatures, and my first thought was: "If I light the fire now the smoke will go toward him and that would not be polite." So, I just stood there and acknowledged him.

Now, polite is an interesting word to use at a time like this but I do have an immense respect for these magnificent creatures and did not want to inconvenience him. As I took in the serene energy of the moment, I felt connected to the elephant and everything around him. As that connection deepened, I noticed that there was a deer-sized antelope, a Bushbuck, standing a little behind the Elephant. He too was calmly observing me.

Neither animal seemed perturbed by my presence. Nor did I feel scared or worried in any way. It was beautiful, we were just one.

My senses were heightened, the beauty of the trees, the sights, sounds and smells abounding. Everything was intensified.

Soon a family of warthogs came trotting down the path for their regular sundowner at the river. They, too, were not bothered by me and passed so close that one brushed my leg as it went by. It felt surreal to be so close to such magnificent animals, to belong there and be connected by nature. It was as if there was a magic spell in existence.

Before long, I heard a loud chattering and creaking of branches behind me. I turned to notice a troop of Baboons noisily making their way to their nightly roosting site.

As the dusk started to intensify and night edged even closer the elephant casually turned away and melted into the bush along with the Bushbuck. It really is incredible how such a formidably large creature can disappear so quickly and silently.

I was spellbound.

In awe, I ran through everything that had just happened. The beauty of the moment, the colors, the intensity of all my senses and the sense of peaceful connection I'd experienced and still felt.

With this indelible memory racing throughout my body, I returned to the kitchen to share the moment with Roy:

"You don't know what you just missed," I said.

Principles In Action

You can see from this story the **three principles of A.A.C.** in action:

I became aware of the elephant less than ten feet away and that it was wonderful. I accepted that he was there, so close. Doing so allowed me to make the conscious choice to be unafraid in any way--to just be. In return I was rewarded with the most wonderful sense of 'being' that this delightful experience gave me.

Wow! What a beautiful moment in my life.

Had I allowed my emotions to be triggered by the sight of the elephant, the end result would have been very different. But I didn't. I simply applied A.A.C.

This is the type of awesome power you have at your disposal once you fully take on board the principles of Awareness, Acceptance and Choice.

A Silent 'Ghost'

Now, not everybody may have the desire to spend time in the wilds of Africa or get so close to wild animals. So let me relate another incident that is much closer to home, yet still evoked a beautiful moment through the power of Awareness, Acceptance and Choice.

I was recently on an overseas Zoom call, and it was the early hours of the morning for me.

As I was talking to my colleague I happened to glance to my right and noticed a 'body' that had appeared from nowhere. It was so sudden, so silent and so unexpected that I called out in fright. *"Aaaargh!"* I shouted before noticing that the ghostly presence that had suddenly materialized was my eldest daughter, Belle.

She should have been fast asleep in bed. Somehow though, she had managed to silently float down the stairs and through the closed door to my study before appearing like a wraith next to me. So total was the silence and so unexpected the incident, it genuinely gave me a fright.

Who knows what my colleague was thinking because the virtual background from Zoom hid the reality of what had happened. All he saw was me looking down and screaming out loud - his poor ears!

I quickly scooped Belle up and she fell asleep in my arms with a smile on her face. She was happy to be close to me and pleased that she'd given daddy a fright. After explaining to my colleague what had happened, we had a good giggle and finished our call on a much happier note.

Once again, you can see the power that Awareness, Acceptance and Choice have. Once I'd got over the initial shock and was aware of what had happened, I accepted it without reservation and made the choice to go on in a happier mood.

Now, here's the thing, I am sure some people would have reacted negatively to the incident. Perhaps they'd have shouted out *"What are you doing here? You're supposed to be in bed, asleep!"* as they allowed the initial incident to trigger anger and embarrassment at the fright they'd shown in public. If they allowed that emotion to take over, what a sad result that would have made.

You Always Have Choice

The above examples show how applying the principles of A.A.C. gives you power. The truth is you always have a choice in the way you react to any situation. Exercising that choice allows you to be happy (if you want) and that being happy is actually a choice you make anyway.

Applying A.A.C. in life is a simple process but it does require practice to make it automatic.

- Develop the **AWARENESS** of what is happening both inside and out
- Take a 'step back', breathe and **ACCEPT** that 'it' is happening
- Once you've done that, you have given yourself the space and power to consciously **CHOOSE** how you react to the situation

Practice A.A.C. Every Day. Make It Your Habit.

If you discover you are already being controlled by emotion then notice that you've just exercised AWARENESS in action and...

That's wonderful!

Now you can move to the **'ACCEPTANCE'** phase as you continue the process.

Because when you do, the emotions will cede their power to you and that is wonderfully liberating.

Michelle Smith is an interfaith minister, energy healing practitioner, and clinical hypnotherapist with a specialization in perinatal health, trauma, grief, and loss. Known for the soothing sound of her voice and calming presence, childbirth education and labor support are passions of Michelle's.

As a doula and midwifery assistant, she's been blessed to attend 750+ births and counting since formally training in 2000.

Michelle founded the Birth Ease Method™ guided relaxation childbirth program and is a birth hypnosis specialist. She is honored to be a member of the Calm Birth leadership team and to help with the creation of meditations for pregnancy and parenting as well for healing after perinatal loss.

Michelle is a professional midwife of thanatology (death midwife) and a certified Grief Educator trained directly by David Kessler—the World's Leading Grief Expert. Michelle is also a teacher with The Institute for the Study of Birth, Breath, and Death.

As the host of The Birth Ease Podcast and the Birth Ease Loss Support podcast, she's featured incredible experts on her podcasts from Jennie Joseph, Sabia Wade, Heidi Snyderburn, and Cristen Pascucci to Heidi Faith and Amy

Wright Glenn. Between her two podcasts, she has gathered a library of knowledge for her listeners, which includes parents and professionals alike.

Contact Michelle:
Email: Michelle@birtheaseservices.com
Website: https://www.birtheaseservices.com/
Facebook: @thebirtheasepodcast,
@birtheaselosssupport
Instagram: @birtheasemichellesmith,
@birtheaselosssupport
LinkedIn: Birth Ease Michelle Smith

SACRED THRESHOLD
BY MICHELLE SMITH

The first thing we do upon leaving our mother's body is breathe in, and the last thing we do upon exiting this world is breathe out. The breath is the link, the thread. Breath is a powerfully loyal friend throughout life's journey between birth and death. ~ Amy Wright Glenn

THE GUARANTEE

In life, there are two sacred thresholds that everyone passes through — birth and death. We are all born, and we will all one day, die. Although they are universal, these shared life transitions can bring fear for many people. Maybe that is because at death and at birth we are faced with the fragility of life.

PRECIOUS SOUNDS

Pregnancy is usually surrounded by joy and anticipation. The promise of life continuing itself. Yet, deep within us, perhaps we know that it is not guaranteed.

The whole room breathes a collective sigh of relief when a baby takes their first breath outside the womb and lets out a big cry. Parents' tears flow in response to that sound. Those first cries newborns make are very distinctive, just as women can make very distinctive sounds in labor, especially when their baby is within moments of birth.

Those of us that attend births know these tale-tell vocalizations.

The changes in her voice and in her breath are our cues that soon her baby will transition into the world from their watery environment in the womb.

There is also a distinct sound that someone can make when they are deep in grief and shock at the loss of a loved one. It is often called the death wail. If you have ever heard someone make it, it is a sound that you will likely never forget.

There are some who say that our bodies know how to give birth and our bodies know how to grieve.

This is something I believe to be true.

Unfortunately, in many ways, this wisdom has become eroded in our fast-paced world. Pregnant people's labors are often induced or augmented to speed things up. The bereaved are expected to be finished grieving after a few weeks or even within days of the funeral. Yet, this is not the rhythm of birth and grief. There is an ebb and flow.

Many people compare labor contractions to waves that rush in, and through, and over them. As the wave ebbs away, it leaves her birthing body more open. As labor progresses, the waves become longer, stronger, closer together. Once the baby is born, the waves will become infrequent and much less intense over the course of the next few days.

In grief, people often say the pain of loss feels like tidal waves threatening to consume them and they may drown. With time, those waves will also become less intense and more manageable. However, a huge wave of grief can still hit from behind when we least expect it.

In both birth and grief, this ebb and flow has a wisdom and assists in healing, although during intense moments of birth or grief, it may not feel that way at all.

A retired midwife friend of mine says that there is a moment when a heart begins to beat and there is the moment that that heart will stop beating. No one knows when that moment will be...

THE LIFE AND DEATH EXPERIENCE

It's early Thanksgiving morning, and we are walking. Crystal has been laboring off and on for a few days with her second baby. She's getting frustrated and tired. Isn't this labor supposed to go more quickly? The contractions have been present, but sporadic for the last 3 days. They are still a bit irregular, but they are getting closer and feeling different.

We all had met at the birth center at 5:20 am. Our midwife, Elena, had checked Crystal's cervix, she was 4 cm dilated (she needs/needed to be 10 cm dilated to be able to begin pushing and give birth to her baby), and Elena helped to stretch her cervix a bit. Elena and I agreed that to get these contractions stronger and more productive, powerwalking for 2 hours would be the best way to do it.

While Crystal's partner rests (I'd suggested to them that he try to get a little sleep, as Crystal will really need his help after the baby is born and they are back home from the birth center), Crystal and I walk, we talk, and we laugh.

The two of us are very happy and grateful that I am her doula* for this birth. With her first baby, I was her childbirth educator, but she had already hired another doula before we met. We grew very close during our classes, and we stayed in touch over the years after her daughter's birth. As we continue walking and enjoying each other's company, we are relieved the contractions are really picking up.

Thanksgiving seems like a lovely day for a baby to be born.

We walk for 90 minutes, and we are all hoping for good news when we return to the birthing room. At 7 am, Elena checks Crystal's cervix once again and she is 7cm dilated! She has moved from active labor to transition. This phase of labor is often the shortest but the most intense.

Crystal is having a waterbirth. Being in the water makes this part of labor more comfortable and she lets us know she is more than ready be in the tub. While the water is running, Elena supports Crystal through her contractions, their hands tightly clasped, and their gazes locked—what is being shared between these two women is nothing short of reverent.

As Crystal relaxes in the water, with her locs pulled up on top of her head, she looks beautiful. She is regal and poised as she gently breathes through the contractions. I remind her to soften her forehead, drop her shoulders and relax her jaw, release her bottom, and meet each contraction with her breath.

The room is serene and filled with the power and energy of birth. Crystal shares with our midwife that her labor is feeling almost ecstatic.

At 8 am, Elena is going off shift. She introduces us to our new midwife Connie, who is lovely. We all chat a bit and settle in with this change as labor intensifies. The two midwives leave the bathroom, and Crystal and I continue to labor.

"Release, relax, and let everything go. Let this contraction rush in and through and over you. Meet it with your breath," I say to Crystal in a low, soft tone, grateful that she finds my voice soothing and grounding.

At 8:35 am Elena comes back into the bathroom. Crystal and I each give her a big hug, and the three of us reluctantly say goodbye to each other. As Elena walks through the birth room, she sees Crystal's phone ringing on the bed and notices it reads, "Ma". She considers picking it up and bringing it to Crystal. She's in labor, I will give her space, Elena decides. She will get to it later once the baby is born.

Crystal's phone rings again a few minutes later. She recognizes the ringtone as her father's. "My brother probably told him I am in labor. It is too much to talk right now. I will call him back once the baby is born," she tells me.

When it rings for the third time, she asks me to get her phone in case the call is about her 6-year-old daughter who is not there with us.

The voice on the other line says, "I know you are in labor, but you need to call your dad. He has been trying to reach you. It's about your mom."

She dials her father's number as the contractions grow stronger and closer together. She places the phone on speaker so I can hold it for her without it falling into the water or getting wet as she talks and manages the contractions.

When her father answers, through his tears he tells Crystal that he found her mom unresponsive and not breathing this morning. He administered CPR to resuscitate her, to no avail. As they talk, we can hear the paramedics working on her mom in the background. The sounds in the room are transporting me back to witnessing my mother-in-law being resuscitated.

The strength that women possess is incredible! As Crystal listens to her father, trying to understand what he is saying and what has happened to her mother, the contractions surge through her body.

This news is so unexpected. Her mother is in good health overall. She calmly comforts her distraught father, quietly breathing through the waves of contractions. Crystal reminds him that the paramedics are there, perhaps they will be able to resuscitate her mom, and her father says he thinks the paramedics may have found a pulse.

Crystal listens to her dad as he wraps his mind around what has happened and is currently going on around him. Throughout the phone call, he's saying over and over, "I don't understand, she doesn't really have any major health issues, just her reflux was bothering her."

Crystal tries to tell him that she is in labor but in this moment the fog of shock weighs heavily upon him and he's unable to comprehend what she's saying. She asks if her brother has made it there yet, and her father replies, "No, but he will be here any minute."

This time when she repeats that she is in labor, the words seem to reach him through the haze, though his voice sounds miles away as he registers them. He hangs up the phone with reluctance.

Crystal and I look at each other wordlessly as we absorb what her father just told her.

In the next moment, our new midwife Connie, comes into the room to check Crystal's vitals and listen to the baby's heart tone. Crystal begins sharing the details of the phone call with her, while I get up to get Crystal's partner from the other room. He is awake, having overheard most of the phone call.

We come back into the bathroom. I retake my spot on the floor next to the tub, and Crystal fills him in about her mom. He sits down behind me and starts tearing up. She is understandably annoyed that he didn't come support her when he overheard her father's distraught voice.

As I continue supporting Crystal through the contractions, I get the inexplicable sense that her mother has just passed away or they will be pronouncing her dead after attempting to resuscitate her.

I look down at my phone; it is 8:56 am.

While Crystal explains everything, the contractions naturally lessened and slowed. The body is wise —it's given her space to call her brother. Crystal asks for her phone, and when he answers, the despair in her brother's voice is unmistakable.

"She's gone, Crystal. They won't let me in to see her. Oh my God, she's gone!"

A couple of tears run down her face as she hears his words. They continue talking, and I'm in awe of my client as she manages to comfort her brother as she did her father through her contractions.

Most women are unable to speak during their contractions or even between them at this point of labor, much less console someone when the shock is also her own.

As her brother begins to regain his composure, the recognition hits him that she's in labor. He sniffles and says, "Okay, baby, go focus on the baby."

We are all stunned beyond words. Crystal's partner drops his head in his hands as he breaks down, sobbing uncontrollably. Just six months ago, a family member died tragically, and he lost his father due to COVID-19.

This morning was the first time that he and I met one another. We only spoke a few words before he accepted the invitation to sleep.

I am sitting on the floor beside the tub facing Crystal, he is sitting behind me. I place my hand on his leg hoping to comfort him as I focus on supporting Crystal through her contractions as well as her own shock and heartache at the death of her mother, as she readies herself to give birth and become a mother for the second time.

I take a breath. I keep my presence calm, soothing, and steady.

My role is to hold space for the intensity of birth and death, shock, and grief, and the welcoming of new life all occurring within the same moments.

At 9:15 am Connie needs to take another set of vitals. After she finishes, she shares that she has heard it said that as one soul dies and another is born, their spirits greet and pass one another as they move from one plane of existence to another. It is comforting to think that perhaps grandma greeted her grandson as he prepares to be born.

At 8:57 am Crystal's mother was pronounced dead, and at 9:57 am Crystal is pushing.

Her son is born into her hands at 10:06 am.

BIRTH, BREATH, AND DEATH

Birth, Breath, and Death are inextricably entwined in these moments.

The last breath and the death of this child's grandmother as her child, his mother, deliberately focuses on her own breath as she labors to bring him earthside. The shock and sorrow of the situation softens temporarily as we witness the sanctity of birth. Seeing him take his first breath, hearing his cries, taking in his perfection is a balm on our hearts.

These are the **Sacred Thresholds—Birth, Breath, and Death**, the ones I have been called to hold space for. To do so, "I stay fully present for a person's experience no matter how intense. I provide a compassionate, non-judgmental presence. I validate. I honor what is. I comfort. I guide."

I listen deeply.

Now I have attended births where everything goes beautifully and smoothly, and I have attended births that were extremely difficult. In some, the baby was miscarried or stillborn.

I've had a client's father admitted into hospice the same day she went into labor. But never have I had a client discover, while laboring, that their parent, their mother, had died.

Elena, our first midwife, told me later that day that Crystal chose well having me as her doula without even knowing it.

We are all grateful that I am someone who walks between these two worlds of birth and death.

For me, and many others, they are two sides of the same coin that is life. Sides that are connected through our breath.

*Doula — a birth professional that provides non-medical, educational, emotional, and physical support during pregnancy, birth, and postpartum.

Tammy Rader is a contributing and #1 International Best-Selling Author in *The Cinderella Monologues* and is an emerging speaker.

She is a Cancer survivor and mentor, very focused on guiding those with cancer through, and beyond their journey to triumph.

Having been diagnosed just 39 days apart with both Breast and Rectal cancer, Tammy is now a *"Thriver,"* who finds resilience with the help of humor, practicing mindset, and having gratitude.

Tammy currently lives in Edmonton, Alberta, Canada. She is the Founder of ***BeYOUtiful Beyond Your Diagnosis (by Tam)*** and has programs, courses, group, and one-on-one talks. She will be including retreats among other exciting events.

She loves the simple little things in life, like going for walks, the sound of laughter, ladybugs, unicorns, and flip flops.

Contact Tammy:

Website: www.beyoutiful.health.com *(please be aware of spelling, auto correct wants to change it - beYOUtiful)*

Email: Tammy@beyoutiful.health

LinkedIn: linkedin.com/in/tammyrader

Facebook: facebook.com/tammy.rader.35

Instagram: instagram.com/tammy.rader73

WHY ME?. . .WHY NOT ME?
BY TAMMY RADER

The limit does not exist. ~ Kathleen Cameron

"Even though I know that I'm not going to feel what I want to feel and that makes me quite anxious, I'm still learning to love, honor and accept myself in this new state, in this new body and everything will be okay!"

These are the words that I started saying to myself after receiving a life-altering diagnosis. I had and will have, many changes and adjustments to make, during this journey. This disease took so much from me and yet, oddly enough, gave me so much.

I was born in Ontario, Canada and grew up in a little, tiny village called Dashwood, where you knew everyone, and they knew you. I've been blessed with - at most times - a wonderful younger brother and the most incredible, loving parents who celebrated their 50th wedding anniversary in 2020! Unfortunately, my dad passed away two weeks shy of their 52nd anniversary. R.I.P. Dad.

I have one son, Steven, I call my little man and is my miracle. At age 16, I was diagnosed with Endometriosis and IBS (Irritable Bowel Syndrome). I was told that I would never have children.

SURPRISE! By the powers that be, I managed to get pregnant. His dad and I got married and I gave birth to my beautiful, brown haired, blue-eyed, little miracle.

My son is my whole world! He has grown into a fine young man, of whom I am very proud! He works hard at his full-time job, working with concrete and does custom designed wood working. He's made some beautiful pieces but the most precious piece he's made is the one-of-a-kind piece he made for me...* ?

Unfortunately, my marriage didn't work out and we ended up in a nasty divorce. It caused a great deal of stress for all of us, but I'm happy to share that today, we are friends. Following that, I did what I had to do, to show and teach my son that no matter what life deals you, you must show up and never give up!

TIME PASSES

It was soon to be my 40th birthday. I headed out west to Alberta, Canada, somewhere I was called to visit. I ended up working there, that's where I met my now, loving partner, David.

After two years of flying in and out while working rotational shifts I bought a house in Edmonton. Two things my mom specifically said NOT to do ... buy a house and meet someone. Sorry mom, you might have known I wasn't going to listen.

Fast forward to 2021, a very cold January morning, if you know Edmonton, Alberta, you know how cold it can get, -40 degrees Celsius and colder. I had just stepped out of the shower, started brushing my long dark hair as my hand grazed across my chest ...What's this?

I immediately did a self-exam and found a lump in my right breast.

Your mind goes "squirrel," and a thousand things come up.

I had been working extra hours, doing painting for the offices upstairs at work, so was I over-using my right arm? Maybe.

The parts or the boxes that I carried: was it too heavy against my chest? Maybe that was the reason.

So many thoughts! Then, no one in my family has breast cancer!

I literally dismissed the possibility for a whole week!

The following Monday, I checked the area again and sure enough, the lump was still there. I called my doctor. She got me in right away for the two necessary tests, a mammogram, and an ultrasound. Those led to biopsies.

I had been telling myself, the lump was nothing, but I think deep down, I knew.

In the middle of the afternoon, at work, (Feb 2021) I received a phone call. The voice on the other end confirmed my worst fear as I was told those three little words, no one ever wants to hear…**"You have cancer."**

There were more things she said during the call, but once I heard those words, nothing else she said made sense! It was like a massive punch to the gut!

Next, the surgeon called and said I had to have a single mastectomy.

I cried.

What am I going to look like? Will my partner still love me?

He explained that I had an aggressive form of Breast Cancer, and they found that it was already in my lymph nodes, in my under arm.

Next came tests, bloodwork, appointments, and a very heartbreaking phone call home to my family.

I had my mastectomy. (March 15, 2021) When I awoke from surgery, I had a blue binding on and two drain tubes coming out of my right side. They took my right breast and also 17 lymph nodes from my armpit!

After a life-altering surgery like that happens, there is an overwhelming number of thoughts, feelings and emotions that go through you.

We take our bandages off and see this new reflection (in the mirror), staring back at us. No One understands just how emotionally strong we now have to become!

I remember being able to finally have a full shower after the mastectomy and I broke down when I felt nothing on my chest. I felt the warm water at the base of my neck and then again on my stomach, at my lower rib cage - no feeling in between.

I will never feel the beautiful feeling of warm, running water over my breast again!

As I'm sobbing in the shower with the sound of the water muffling my cries, I remember what some people said to me, when I told them of the diagnosis and that I had to have a mastectomy.

"Now you get to have a free boob job!"...and more. I'd just like to say, *"screw you!"*

You will **NEVER** understand, and I hope you **never** have to!

AND THE NEWS CONTINUES...

Just **two weeks** after the mastectomy, I was told those three devastating words **AGAIN!**

Can you imagine?

I said earlier that most of my life, I've had IBS and endometriosis. Both are invisible diseases, like most others. Sometimes we are inflamed on the inside but look great on the outside. We go to work and do everyday things without anyone knowing our struggles, how the disease kept us up all night, or the pain we pushed through, like the two car accidents I was in, neither my fault, by the way.

In late 2019, I could feel something wasn't right. I was in a lot of pain; bathroom visits were getting longer. I was constipated my whole life, but things were just becoming "different and difficult", so I called my doctor. Once again, I need to have more tests. You know, you don't get those appointments the next day, so it was booked for spring of 2020.

Well, with the world situation as it was, that appointment did not happen. It was pushed back three times! Thanks, Covid.

Sitting in the specialist's room, waiting for him to wash his hands after giving me an internal exam, the way he looked and the amount of time he was taking, I just knew what he was going to say!

You know that knot in the pit of your stomach when you feel that something just isn't right?

I asked him not to say the words, actually, I BEGGED him NOT to say the words! David (my partner) was in the room the whole time and when the doctor said, *"I'm sorry, I don't have good news."* I said **"NO, please!"** He said, *"You have rectal cancer."*

I lost it and literally, started sobbing, **"How is this my reality? How could this be happening, again?"**

David came over and held me. He had tears in his eyes. I thought, ***what the hell am I going to do?***

Some people hear those words once in a lifetime and some for a second or third time, **IF** *the cancer comes back*, but to hear those same words **SO** close together, was an absolute nightmare! You have no idea!

IT WAS JUST 39 DAYS AFTER I WAS DIAGNOSED WITH BREAST CANCER AND JUST 14 DAYS AFTER MY MASTECTOMY!

I needed a few days to process everything because this is crap!

I'm NOT going down without a fight!

Death is NOT an option!

My perseverance, my resilience, my WANT to live and my ATTITUDE - my mom always says they broke the mold when they made me!

I am stubborn and I am a fighter! It was hard to find positivity in this situation, but I did, and I went from "Why Me?' ... to "*Why NOT Me!*"

My oncology team now had to figure out a new plan. With the newest diagnosis, treatments for my breast had to be put on hold. The Rectal Cancer treatments started first. Enter... 36 radiations and 3 rounds of chemo.

When I first heard the word, radiation, I thought it's "really like a bad sunburn." Well, I'm here to tell you it is the WORST sunburn you can get! You burn from the inside - out.

PSA (Public Service Announcement) here - I'm going to be graphic. I lost four layers of skin from my pubic bone to my tailbone and inside my thighs. I also developed a prolapsed bladder from the radiation. Sweet eh?!

After the treatments for the rectal were done, I received permission to go home to see my family, in Ontario. It had been two years since I was home!

My hair was getting very thin from the chemo and there was a big bald spot at the back of my head.

You know, it's funny, I was more afraid of losing my hair than I was of the chemo.

"People" said, *"It's just hair, it'll grow back."* I felt like shouting at the top of my lungs, ***NO! It's NOT JUST HAIR!***

Please don't **ever** say this to someone who is going through this or losing their hair for any other reason!

It's a **control** thing. Cancer takes **SO** damn much from you! I wanted, no, I **NEEDED** to take control of this! **I wanted to FEEL empowered and let cancer know, who's the boss!**

I'LL DO IT MY WAY, THANK YOU!

The third day I was home, I asked my son, "Will you help me shave my head?" He didn't hesitate for a second. He said, "Yes, I'll even shave mine right after!"

Ahh, my little man.

My best friend and her daughter were coming that day also, so I surprised them and asked if they would be part of this special moment too. They were so happy and honored. No, they didn't shave their heads.

I put what hair I had left, into a ponytail and my son cut it off and then we each took turns shaving my head! It was the most incredible, empowering, beautiful moment!

I still get choked up when I think about it because **I took control!** I didn't let cancer take that from me and it turns out, I looked pretty good bald!

Back to Alberta and time for the treatments for my breast. Six rounds of chemo and 20 radiations. There were complications and more than once, I ended up in the hospital, once for 5 days! For 48 hours, my immune system was ZERO! This was the scariest moment, so far in this frightening journey. I didn't know if I would ever be home again.

Turns out, I was administered too much chemo. When they mix the solution, it's supposed to be made to fit you, specifically. Your age, height, weight, the type of cancer you have, the stage and grade all matter and go into the concoction.

Luckily, they got it right for the next dose though.

I finished all my treatments, February 1, 2022, and I got to ring my third and final bell!

When you are finished with a series of treatments, you ring a bell. It signifies THIS part of the journey is over.

Most people only ring one bell, I rang three!

I've always said, I wanted to help people and I never knew what that looked like...until now.

I'm starting a new chapter.

My mission is to help people who are in the beginning, middle or finished treatment. Whatever stage they are in, I want to help them take the next step in LIVING.

I felt so alone most of my journey. My family lives almost 3000 miles away and when we talked, they tried, but they just didn't understand some of the things I was saying or how I was really feeling. Neither did David, my partner.

How could they?

I don't want anyone else to feel this way! Cancer sucks! It's a lonely disease but it doesn't have to be!

For me, I turned my "Why Me?" into "Why NOT Me!"

There are so many things you can do and one thing - even though it's hard at times - is keeping a positive attitude. It gets you so much further in life!

Don't get me wrong, there were **many** dark days, and still are, unfortunately, and there were times at night when I was afraid to fall asleep because I didn't know if I was going to wake up.

Having a positive outlook, saying affirmations, drawing up a vision board (yeah, some people thought that idea was crazy) using coping mechanisms and being a little bit stubborn *(ok, maybe a lot)*, really helped me get through the darkest times.

I'm a "cup half full kinda gal." So, if you or someone you know has just been told those three devastating words...and aren't sure what to do or where to turn, I'm here!

*The custom, one-of-a-kind wood piece my son made me; a large, thick chunk of wood with live edges, (the bark is still on) he planed it down and carved a large cancer ribbon in the middle of it. He filled the ribbon with two colors of epoxy, blue and pink. In the middle at the top, he inserted half of the staples from my mastectomy and placed them in the shape of a heart. (30 staples total)

It's the most beautiful gift I have ever received! He truly is my whole world and one of the MANY reasons I fought (and still fight) for my life! I will never again think I can't conquer something because look at me - here I am, conquering this! Cancer may have started this fight but I'm going to finish it!

Gina Catherine Vanderham is passionate to create psychologically healthy workplaces, helping executives, managers and their employees remove stigma and improve their mental health to live happier and healthier lives.

She is a Substance Abuse Professional with the US Department of Transportation and an Internationally Certified Alcohol and Drug Counsellor, registered with the Canadian Addiction Counsellors Certification Board. She is also a Certified Employee Assistance Professional and registered with the Employee Assistance Professional's Association.

Gina holds the designation as a Clinical Member of the American Association of Marriage, Family and Child Therapists, as well as a master's degree in Counselling Psychology and a Certificate in Chemical Dependency. She has received post master's training in critical incident stress debriefing and dealing with trauma in the workplace, organizational development, disability management, occupational safety, psychological safety and many more areas too numerous to mention.

She also holds certificates in various spiritual and healing techniques including Eye Movement Desensitization Reprocessing (EMDR), Clinical Hypnosis, Therapeutic touch, Reiki, Spiritual Direction, and Addiction Counselling.

Gina has treated thousands of individuals over the past 30 years who had addiction issues. She has worked with individuals in different organizations both in Canada and the United States.

Some of Gina's speaking engagements include the British Columbia Society of Mediators on "The Effects of Alcohol and Drugs in Mediation Clients", the Employee Assistance Professionals Association on "Addiction in the Workplace", and the Working Together Conference on "Youth and Eating Disorders" and "Burnout in the Professional Counsellor

Contact Gina:
Website: www.ginavanderham.com
Email: ginavanderham@gmail.com
Linkedin: https://www.linkedin.com/in/gina-vanderham-ma-mft-icadc-sap-rcc-phsa-b544051/?originalSubdomain=ca

ADDICTION IN YOUR WORKPLACE?
BY GINA CATHERINE VANDERHAM, M.A.

One thing you must realize is that: you either kill your addiction or your addiction will eventually kill you.
~ Oche Otorkpa

"But for the Grace of God, Go I..." A paraphrase from St. Paul in the Bible.

Addiction, regardless to what, is most often a symptom of a person seeking *relief from the pain* they are feeling. And then there is the stimulation of the *reward systems in the brain.*

Addiction in the workplace is detrimental in many regards.

Firstly, to the person who finds themselves experiencing addiction, it is cause for shame, guilt, embarrassment, and sub-par performance.

Secondly, one who is addicted doesn't have the sober capacity to make accurate judgement calls, adhere to safety rules and regulations, or react appropriately in dangerous situations, all of which can result in tragedies that may well have been avoided.

Thirdly, the employer may not even recognize or understand that their employee has a problem that often affects everyone around them, as well as the profits.

I know these things to be true, as I have unique education and experience in this area. I hold a master's degree in counselling psychology, am an Approved Substance Abuse Professional, an Internationally Certified Alcohol and Drug Counsellor, as well as being a Certified Employee

Assistance Professional. In addition, I have numerous supporting certifications and credentials.

MY STORY

I wish I could say I have always done this work and been a contributing member of society. Sadly, that would be untrue.

Did I mention that I was an addict? Maybe I missed that part.

Yes, indeed I was addicted to alcohol and numerous other drugs. I became a very lost sheep. I held various jobs during this time and was not so helpful to my employers and fellow employees. I was absent, or not present when at work because of my alcohol and drug use. It's called "presenteeism."

There are so many factors that increase one's vulnerability to addiction. Unfortunately, I had several of them.

I was born into a family that had dysfunction like the vast majority of the families in this world, regardless of where they live, their race, economic status, religion, or gender. You get the picture.

Like a whole lot of people, I suffered emotional, physical, and sexual trauma throughout my formative years, inside my family, with and others later on.

100% of the addicts I have seen in my practice over the last 30 years, have come from dysfunctional families, and have suffered trauma in their lives.

Around the age of 13, I turned to alcohol and smoking cigarettes to ease the pain of my shame, depression, and anxiety. I believe most addicts are shamed based. The abuse happened to them, but they take on the shame of the abuser. They are made to think that it's their fault, that they're bad, the blame rests upon them and not where it should – upon the perpetrator!

I began working at the tender age of 12 delivering newspapers. At 16, I went to work at a drycleaning store. The supervisor turned out to be a drug dealer who introduced me to marijuana (now called cannabis), and I quickly became a regular customer.

Are you surprised to learn that one of my very first experiences in the workplace was the source, the ultimate birth of my heavy using, and my financial problems?

My hard-earned money now had to go to funding my habit.

We have become an addicted society. Addiction is so common – about 40% of us have problematic misuse of some substance or activity and have problems in our lives because of our addictions.

Whether it is an addiction to drugs, alcohol, gambling, people, food, or sex, just to name a few, getting it is the top priority. Much time is lost to thinking about planning, seeking, finding, using, and then recovering from the hangover from the drug of choice, which makes you go out and do it all over again.

Addiction can be understood as continued substance misuse despite negative consequences and loss of control. Lifelong legal troubles can also be very much part of the addiction. Just consider the incarceration population!

I failed to graduate high school. Things didn't look good.

Every job I had was adversely affected by my addictions. While I never stole money, I took from them in many other ways, such as not being fully present to do my job properly, absenteeism, company supplies including food, time spent on non-work-related activities such as internet resources, and so much more. These are things that many do not see as stealing from their employers.

At the time, I was vaguely aware that these things were wrong, but the more I used, true to addict form, the more my values and sense of morality, went by the wayside. Nothing was more important to me than getting my fix. And the shame grew.

Because I came to do this work through suffering addiction personally, it is important to me to give back and to help those in organizations and employees, who are suffering as I did. We spend so much of our time at work, the workplace should become a highly effective place for intervention, help and recovery.

My specialization is in *helping management to recognize* addiction. I teach them how to document a situation and how to have the tough conversations with those afflicted, so that both have a positive result, which ultimately should be a healthy, recovering addict who returns to work, able to be an asset to the business they work for.

Did you know that in some places a business, including owners and managers, can be criminally charged for not performing due diligence in creating and maintaining an occupationally and psychologically safe work environment?

PREVENT AND PREPARE! Structures need to be in place and ready to be utilized when trouble strikes.

THE STIGMA IS SHAMING

My passion is to decrease stigma around addiction and mental health issues. There is *no shame* in having an addiction: it is a mental health/medical condition.

No one ever wakes up and says, "Gee, I'd like to be an addict."

The concern should be what happened to you (compassion), not what's wrong with you (judgement/shaming).

We may not be responsible for the addiction, but we are responsible for our recovery. It takes great strength, support, and resources to succeed at recovery.

I worked for a major oil company as a secretary. My boss was a great guy and a lot of fun. He drank a lot. He would go out at lunch and come back even happier and more jovial, with a redder face and a wobble in his walk. Not a word was spoken about it.

During this job I was sad and near the end of my own addiction. I wish someone at this massive company had helped. Obviously, my boss was not the one to do so. If only, someone would have left me a card or brochure that read: If you are feeling depressed, are drinking too much, feeling isolated at work, call 1-800-we-can-help.

NEEDED SERVICES AT WORK

Employee Assistance Programs (EAPs) have their origins in the late 1930s. They were formed out of programs that dealt with occupational alcoholism. During a time when drinking on the job was the norm, people noticed the effects it had on job performance and productivity and decided it best to offer help.

Currently, EAPs are no longer the referral of choice. A specialized referral to an occupational health doctor should be the standard. These professionals who specialize in addiction are qualified to make recommendations about treatment, follow-up after care, and monitoring agreements, ensuring the employee is and continues to be, fit to return to work.

Peer programs are also proving to be helpful these days in getting the person with the addiction or mental health issue the help they need.

Jobs are adversely affected by addiction in different ways - not being fully present to do the job, absenteeism, siphoning off company supplies including food, using time at work on non-work-related activities, etc. In general, the more an addict uses, the more their self-esteem, values and sense of morality suffer.

With these and other troubles accumulating, the disease of addiction eventually leads the addict to isolate more and more, to hide their using, and to feel worse and worse about themselves.

It's funny they call it recovery, because often people are not recovering skills, they are *developing* new ones, such as stress management or social skills. Addicts in active addictions don't process feelings, they just drink them into oblivion. The problems don't go away. They must be resolved in a conscious and responsible way.

INTERVENTIONS AND BEYOND

When my sisters did my **intervention** – the range of emotions I felt were vast and not all of them happy.

However, I followed through. I was fortunate enough to learn, being brought up Roman Catholic, that God loved me unconditionally. I believed God was working through them.

Their loving suggestion came at the right time, as I was beginning to see that Alcoholism was afflicting me. Through one of my sister's friends who had worked for the School Board, I accessed the appropriate services. I attended a reputable counselling agency, went to detox, and then a 28-day treatment program and followed up with aftercare.

Treatment definitely held its challenges for me. Adjusting to dealing with my emotions and other people in group therapy wasn't easy. I thought I could never give up drinking. I thought I could never go a year! So, I went one day at a time. Luckily, I had support. I frequently wanted to leave the group treatment. My dear grandmother passed away while I was attending treatment, and I was not allowed to attend her funeral. Most treatment centres are very strict.

When I left treatment, I had to change my circle of friends. Had I not parted company, I may have started drinking again. I didn't need the temptation. I was starting to make better conscious decisions for staying clean and sober and improving my life in the areas of career, family, etc. I returned to my local university and completed my bachelor's degree in psychology. For a while, I worked as a financial planner, but something was missing - it was not my passion.

Early in recovery, I became pregnant. The relationship I was in was toxic and as it and I were both unstable, I gave up my son for adoption. It was one of the hardest decisions of my life and the most painful. I knew in my heart that it was the best option for him.

The poem called **Footprints** was on the hospital wall - its message struck me deeply. I've included it at the end of this chapter. Maybe it will help you or someone you know.

Grief is a very difficult emotion to hold, and when you're not used to feeling any of your feelings, it can be overwhelming. It can be stuffed away but it will resurface when you might least expect it.

When it was time to be choosing a career, I wanted to go back to school. I decided to become a psychotherapist helping others with addiction in private therapy. For 30 years I have specialized in addiction and have helped thousands of people recover. I've worked in treatment centers, inpatient and outpatient facilities, drinking driving programs, and in groups for children of alcoholics, as well as with troubled teens, on crisis lines, and at an outpatient clinic for several years before starting my own private practice.

SUFFERING IN THE WORKPLACE

Please help make your workplace **a resource for your employees suffering from addiction**.

Help is available and recovery is not only possible but can be reality.

I worked extensively with the United States Department of Transportation for many years as a Substance Abuse Professional, interviewing, assessing, and then prescribing treatment or education to employees who tested positive on random tests for substance use.

These people had many different reactions to being in my office. Some were grateful that their company had a policy and had come forward to get help. Some were angry, some in denial and some lied to me, themselves, and everyone else. **I've seen people in denial after receiving 11 drinking and driving charges, still blaming the police!**

It's nearly unfathomable for some people to admit they have a problem because then they would have to do something about it. The underlying shame is overwhelming and so the defense of **denial** settles in.

I've seen people choose alcohol over their family and much-loved children, to where their children have become wards of the government and child protection programs. How sad.

May there be no doubt: Addiction is a chronic, complex, fatal, and progressive disorder most often resulting in tragic circumstances.

There is still a huge amount of stigma in our culture that prevents people suffering from addiction from getting well. It is my hope that this chapter has given you some understanding about addiction and compassion for the addict.

I further hope that the workplace can become a better-informed arena for its employees, that they may recover in a compassionate system of understanding people.

And I'm here to help.

Footprints In The Sand

One night a man had a dream. He dreamed
he was walking along the beach with the LORD.

Across the sky flashed scenes from his life.
For each scene he noticed two sets of
footprints in the sand: one belonging
to him, and the other to the LORD.

When the last scene of his life flashed before him,
he looked back at the footprints in the sand.

He noticed that many times along the path of
his life there was only one set of footprints.

He also noticed that it happened at the very
lowest and saddest times in his life.

This really bothered him and he
questioned the LORD about it:

"LORD, you said that once I decided to follow
you, you'd walk with me all the way.
But I have noticed that during the most
troublesome times in my life,
there is only one set of footprints.
I don't understand why when
I needed you most you would leave me."

The LORD replied:

"My son, my precious child,
I love you and I would never leave you.
During your times of trial and suffering,
when you see only one set of footprints,
it was then that I carried you."

Author: Carolyn Joyce Carty

Mila Johansen is a public speaker, writing and publishing coach, teacher, and writer.

She is the best-selling author of seven books, including, *From Cowgirl to Congress*: *Journey of a Suffragist on the Front Lines*, a first-person account from Jessie Haver Butler, Mila's grandmother who put together the Pulitzer School of Journalism, was the first woman lobbyist in D.C. and taught public speaking to Eleanor Roosevelt.

Mila also has several more books in progress and loves to write and produce short screenplays. She has developed "The Short Book" concept giving people all over the world permission to write their "short book" first.

Contact Mila:
milajohansen.com

BEAT THE B*TCHES
BY MILA JOHANSEN

Butterflies can't see their wings. They can't see how truly beautiful they are, but everyone else can. People are like that as well. -Unknown

After my third year in college at Chico State, I found myself in the presence of a real live, bone-fide goddess--Jane Fonda. Yep. And she lived up to all the major requirements it takes to be classified as a "goddess". Every box was checked: Gracious-check; Beautiful-check; Intelligent-check; Successful-check; Generous-double check and so on.

My famous suffragist, speaker grandmother, Jessie Haver Butler, who taught public speaking to Eleanor Roosevelt, was invited several times to share the podium in Hollywood with Gloria Steinem and Marlo Thomas as the elder suffragette. She was in her early 90s and often took me along. That is where I met Jane Fonda, who sometimes attended the events.

Hired as a camp counselor, I found myself surrounded by a mix of famous political fanatics and Hollywood royalty. Jane, married to Tom Hayden, one of the Chicago Seven, donated her Santa Barbara Hills hideaway for an innovative summer camp for kids. The organizers filled the cabins with children gathered from the Cesar Chavez work fields to mix with offspring of the Hollywood elite.

Three women ran the camp, each pretty and in, what appeared to be, great physical shape: one blond, one brunette and the last with raven, black hair. Recruited from their normal environment in the political arena orchestrating Tom Hayden's legislative career, the triangle of women found themselves surrounded by a menagerie of perplexing children and outspoken camp counselors. Probably more suited to the battlefield of politics, they often seemed like fish flopping frantically out of water. Our new "bosses" ran copious meetings, as if we were part of their political campaign, which we found out later, we were expected to join.

The warning came at me from every possible angle. First from the camp nurse, then our chef, and afterwards, each camp counselor chimed in. "Oh, you have Jane's daughter, Vanessa." "Watch out, last summer, she was the terror of every counselor and ran the camp." "Uh oh, I feel sorry for you." I half expected Vanessa, age ten, to show up in a military uniform with whip in hand.

Glad to have the warning, I prepared myself for the coming conflict. I pulled out my most powerful weapon . . . a book called "Hope For The Flowers."

The children arrived by bus or were dropped off by parents. Everyone gathered on the front lawn waiting for cabin assignments. We each marched our small group of eight to the waiting bunk beds.

Not sure how I knew to do it, I sat my excited group of 4th and 5th graders in a circle on the floor and began reading about the lowly caterpillar turning into a chrysalis, and finally into a beautiful floating butterfly. I had them at "caterpillar".

Each week, when the new attendees arrived, we were expected to create a skit for our charges to perform that first night. I could tell right away that Vanessa possessed an extraordinary amount of talent in the acting department. Together, we created a unique, smart mini play starring the precocious young actress. She basked in the part and worshiped me from then on. Using a colorful parachute, I had brought with me, our little skit showed substance compared with the mundane, over-used, typical camp fare the other groups resorted to.

I'm sure the higher ups were encouraged that night that they hired the right person to head up the drama portion of the camp. I spent most days teaching theatre games to the different aged groups sent to me. The kids loved playing games and I became very popular.

About once a week, a Hollywood actor would visit and take over the class, which allowed me to indulge in some hefty celebrity exposure. People like Peter Riegert from Animal House, Cher, various comedians, and even some musicians. Paul Winter, the famous musician, showed up one week with one of his wolves. The entire camp stood in a giant circle as he came around and let each of us get close to the venerable beast.

Even the chef turned out to be part of the Hollywood elite. In his former life, he worked as one of the head writers on the T.V. show, "Leave it to Beaver". A hard opposite from the man he became, with his wicked, acerbic, gay wit that wafted out of the kitchen and into the dining room, along with the aromas of the gourmet food he prepared.

Thirteen other movie stars lived with us full-time that summer. One of them became my best friend and trusted confidant. Borrowed from the corrals of the Burbank cowboy studio lots, the 13 horses became every camper's favorite pastime. The blonde boss turned out to be an experienced horsewoman and supervised all of our equine events and adventures. We learned to groom, saddle, and ride the willing beasts, who stood still as stone as we practiced our newfound skills on them. Each horse seemed as mellow as a turtle from massive amounts of handling on copious western sets.

Each a famous celebrity in their own right, you can still see their performances in older movies. Two of our equine camp mates doubled as the white horse in "Butch Cassidy and the Sundance Kid". I got to ride both of them.

Then there were the two brown and white horses, Tom and Jerry, that were famous for pulling all sorts of western wagons. Whenever possible I chose Tom to ride and we forged a summer-long friendship.

One glorious day, the blonde boss came up to me and said, "I need you to go along on a horseback camping trip to help me with the kids." Paired with Tom as my equine partner, we rode all thirteen horses up into the hills, for a long three-day adventure. We discovered a large body of water where the humans in the group swam, while the horses drank.

Then moving on, we finally reached our first night's destination at a nearby ranch. I tied Tom to a fence next to where I slept as he stood sentry over me. An equine friend is like no other, warm-bodied, steady, eager to please and easy to get along with. Almost like a large dog that I could ride, Tom ended up being the best part of my summer in the hills of Santa Barbara.

AN UNLIKELY HERO

Too sarcastic to appreciate a wide-eyed neophyte like me, the sardonic chef relished in making cutting jokes at my expense. He was soon joined in this cruel pastime by one of the male camp counselors, a lawyer on hiatus from the court system, parading about as a teacher of children. Together, they tortured their prey—me—mercilessly. I have no idea what prompted this mean treatment except perhaps I was an easy target, raised on Pollyanna, Mary Poppins, and The Wizard of Oz. Not possessing any aptitude for a witty defense, I pretended not to hear them.

But one day, I stunned my two torturers and gained their undying respect. I unwittingly became the unexpected camp hero, worshiped forever-more by the entire staff.

The triangle of women called us all to a meeting. They announced to us that everyone's salaries would be cut by $100.00. from the $1,000.00 promised. (That was a lot of money back then) The reason stated: they needed to raise money for Tom Hayden's campaign for the upcoming election! They expected all of us to comply and gladly give up our hard-earned dollars to the cause. Can you imagine!!!

Shock circled the room when I jolted up and vehemently protested. I have no idea what came over me. I had never spoken up for anything before. I must have been possessed. I stood straight up and said, "No. No. You promised us $1,000.00 for the summer and you will give us the full amount." My voice rang out for the next few minutes in an unintended speech as the entire room stared at me in astonishment.

Later that day, the three dictators called me in to their office and told me that because of my speech, the money would not be taken out of our salaries. I said, "Good. That is the right thing to do."

The next morning, I walked into the kitchen to find the chef and the lawyer offering me a dose of hero worship in their own twisted way. "And here she is . . . the contestant for 'Beat The B*tches'." Conducting an elaborate mock game show right there surrounded by stainless steel appliances, the two made up for all their past "mean girl" tactics. I basked in the newfound role of "Golden Child" and reveled in their acceptance. I became one of them that morning, barefoot on the linoleum, no longer the target of their wicked jokes.

Grateful for my courageous outburst, the entire staff lifted me up and carried me through the streets in triumph. Just kidding. But it felt like that. I often grin in the remembrance of that swift moment of glory.

PLASTER FACES, EARTHQUAKES AND SKINNY DIPPING

Jane Fonda called in a bunch of favors to make the camp happen and to keep things interesting. Art, drama, horseback riding, petting a wolf, swimming, and did I say art?

The Art Diva was a creative force, showing up each week to lead us in various, in-depth adventures of creation. We would lather each kid's face with Vaseline and then apply layers of wet plaster bandage material to make exact replica masks.

Almost a spiritual experience, I've made over 500 for individuals since learning the process from that artistic diva. Why the copious amounts of Vaseline, you might ask? Because if you don't grease the entire surface, eyelashes and other protruding parts will be ripped off when removing the bandage mask once it dries to the perfect shape of each face. **Warning: Don't try this at home without proper training.**

As a trained lifeguard, they posted me at the pool for part of most days, not a hardship since swimming is my passion. One day, as I sat and watched the kids swim, the ground began to shake violently. The water in the pool swished back and forth vigorously, pulling the kids back and forth with it. Swish, swish, swish about eight times, and before I could stand up, the earthquake was over. Thankfully no one had banged against the sides, I cleared the pool in case of a repeat.

Okay, question.

What is summer camp without at least one sneaky maneuver? It's a required camp activity. Right?

So, the week, Vanessa was in my cabin, the girls and I decided it was time to go for a late-night skinny dip. The covert plot thickened as we huddled together in the middle of the floor, planning every aspect of our naughty crusade. Time: midnight when everyone is sleeping. Attire: bathing suit and robe. Oops, nix the bathing suit, this was a naked adventure. Noise: none. Copious amounts of training to be silent and not wake the rest of the camp.

All plans in place, we lined up at 11:55pm, in robes with towels in hand when, all of a sudden, headlights blasted through our window! Jane, returning from Hollywood, opened the door and stared, surprised at the band of girls waiting on the other side. She gasped and asked, "What is going on?"

From somewhere, a flippant voice answered her--my voice. "We are on a mission to go skinny dipping. You are welcome to join us, but if not, please get out of our way."

Obviously taken aback, she moved to the side and said, "Well, okay. I was just wondering why the lights were on in here so late."

She smiled to herself, returned to her car and drove up the hill to her own house. We slipped out the door and tip-toed silently across the grass, sneaking around the building, down to the pool that was just steps from the boy's cabins on the lower level.

I put my finger to my mouth as we reached the concrete. Robes dropped and the girls jumped into the water. Instant cacophony! All training forgotten! Screams of delight pierced the air, and I shuttered knowing that by now the entire camp was awake and knew what we were doing. To my surprise, no one showed up to reprimand us, and no one mentioned it the next day.

BULLIES NOT ALLOWED

Vanessa's half-sister came with her to camp. I intervened several times when she tried to bully Vanessa, which I discovered was a common occurrence. Since I had been bullied many times in my youth, I became very strict when came to bullies.

The first morning in our cabin, I told the girls to each make their own bed. The stepsister looked me squarely in the face and in a very imperious voice said, "I don't make my bed. I have a maid." Stunned, along with half of the campers who were from the Cesar Chavez work camps, I said, "We don't have maids here, you will make your own bed."

She scowled at me. But, in the end, she made her own bed from then on without complaint. She ended up being somewhat of a good sport about things.

ONLY THE CHILDREN

Near the last day of summer camp, I sat, dangling my feet in the pool, when Jane came to sit next to me. She thanked me for helping Vanessa with her stepsister. She told me how the dynamics between the two girls had shifted. I found myself surprised at her generous praise and of course very pleased. I didn't think I had done anything special. I treated all kids in the same fashion wherever I taught.

The last night of camp, my then boyfriend and future husband, Rich, came to pick me up. He and Jane decided to cook dinner for the entire group. They were in the kitchen for hours together having a grand time talking and putting together a delicious meal.

During that time, I walked into the kitchen to find Tom Hayden cleaning fish in the side sink that he and his young son had caught that day. He thanked me for my work with the kids and then asked me if I was planning to come work on his political campaign. Surprised at his assumption, I replied firmly with my newfound, flippant tone, "No. I only came here to work with children. I'm not political."

Who knew that a relatively shy girl would find her voice in such a powerful, beneficial, yet unlikely way?

I now speak once or twice a week on summits and podcasts. I have become just like my grandmother and speak out boldly against Pesticides and Genetically Modified Food. Following in my grandmother's footsteps, I teach and coach public speaking along with writing and publishing. She (Jessie) believed everyone could be taught to speak out and help change the world to become a better place.

https://www.linkedin.com/in/mila-johansen-pentopublished/

Katy Maag is a BSN, RN, CCRP , Certified Stress Management Coach, Uppiness Facilitator, Presenter, and a Laughter Yoga/Therapist Teacher who helps provide tools for stress management and laughter to provide more joy in current times.

Katy works with professionals who want to master their state of wellness. She has been a presenter for over two decades on health and wellness with a side of laughter to add an element of edutainment for a stress tool. She is also one of authors of the bestselling book *Cinderella Monologues.*

Katy believes education and stress management is important for job satisfaction. Working in healthcare has always been stressful but since COVID started it has elevated the stress and disconnect to a new level, never seen before, For this reason, healthcare teams and workers in general are needing tools in order to survive these trying times. Laughter *is a simple and fun tool for connecting teams, reenergizing staff, and reducing stress in the workplace,*

If you or someone you know are looking for a dynamic, extremely knowledgeable, experienced, fun, presenter to help your company, association or organization reduce stress while enhancing their well-being, look no further!

Feel free to contact Katy via:
Website: KMwellnessconsulting.com
Email:1katymaag@gmail.com
Facebook:KMWellness Consulting
Linkedin: KatyMaag

LIVE, LAUGH, & LET IT GO
BY KATY MAAG

You may not control all the events that happen to you, but you can decide not to be reduced by them. ~ *Maya Angelou*

To say my personal life has been a fairytale would be a lie.

I have had an interesting life, though not always easy, it has shaped me to be who I am today. I have either experienced or been a witness to sexual, physical, emotional, and mental abuse from a very young age.

I'm married and have two sons, one of whom has special needs, mentally and physically. I am his primary caregiver. In addition to working, and taking care of my own family, I have been an extended caregiver to others, including my mother and a family friend. I am active in my church, community, and professional organizations.

Through these experiences, I have discovered many things, a few of which, I will share with you in this story.

Like most people, I've dealt with many stressful situations, that I felt at the time, were beyond my control. What was in my control, however, were the choices I made as I navigated the twists and turns that came my way.

As much as most of us would like to, we cannot control the behavior of others. We all have a past, some of it may not be pleasant. More and more, I used laughter as a buffer to get me through stressful and trying times. I still do.

From a very young age, I was overweight and severely bullied because of it. I was a larger girl and often had problems at school because people would say unkind things to, and about me. I would often joke, to cover up the hurt, that there was just more of me to love.

I remember one time when a teammate was upset because our basketball team lost a game. She blamed me because I couldn't perform as quickly as most of the others. Unbeknownst to her, I was still in the changing room and overheard her sharing her opinion about me with a few others. Feeling embarrassed, I decided to stand up for myself. Using laughter as a prelude, I approached her and said, "I prefer if you are going to talk about me, please do so to my face rather than behind my back." She didn't appear to really know how to react, so she laughed awkwardly as well. It may surprise you to learn that we had no problem getting along after that day.

It felt good to stand up for myself, confronting the person and the situation. This was one time when my humor assisted in helping me deal with an unpleasant situation. I believe that laughter helped decrease the tension. This is one of the many times during my childhood when laughter was a mood changer.

HUMOR AND PASSION

Throughout my teenage years, I realized that I really enjoyed helping people. I found that when I did, even with simple tasks, I felt good and so did they.

After high school, one of my first jobs was working in a nursing home. The residents seemed so appreciative and thankful for even the little things I would do with and for them. One fond memory I have is of an elderly gentleman. He had no family or friends nearby. As one can imagine, he felt lonely and often sad.

One evening I was removing his support stockings and had to get down on one knee to do so. I love to sometimes, do silly things, so I jokingly pretended like I was proposing to him, and said "Can I take your hand and help you into slumber land?" He found this to be hilarious! He laughed and laughed. I think he went to sleep in a very happy state that night.

Every time he would see me after that, he would actually giggle! It felt so good to bring a little joy into his and others lives.

We never know how far our kindness ripples out. It was quite some time after I had left my employ at the nursing home when this wonderful man passed away. Imagine my surprise and joy when I opened a letter one day and found that it was from his daughter. She let me know he was gone and expressed her appreciation for the joy I brought to her father.

The time I shared with the nursing home residents, taught me that we not only helped them physically, but we also helped them mentally and emotionally. This was an indicator in my life that showed me I would be a terrific nurse.

Well, it is three decades later, and guess what? I still enjoy being a nurse. I am grateful I found my passion so early in life.

I'm proud to say that my accomplishments in the medical field have been recognized and opened additional career doors for me.

One such accolade offered to me was to become the Nurse of Hope for the American Cancer Society. In this position, I gave presentations to the public about the signs and symptoms of this horrible disease, and when to seek medical advice. This is a very distinguished honor which I am thrilled to say I held for two years.

This was the beginning of what has become my heart song.

Just as in realizing I would be a great nurse, doing presentations as the Nurse of Hope, helped me see that I was talented as a speaker and presenter. I found I can relate to people on their own level while addressing their stress from a professional standpoint.

Stress management is important, more than is often realized or recognized.

In my current position, I facilitate stress management classes for cardiac rehabilitation patients. This is very rewarding. I can see that patients benefit from learning how to cope with their diagnosis, the disease itself, as well as the ongoing living with it. It is most gratifying when they implement the tools and strategies I offer, which give them control in managing their wellness, increasing their energy, and their overall recovery.

One of the tools I teach them is the importance of laughter and humor in their everyday existence.

DARK TIMES

One of the darkest periods of my life happened throughout the last five years. Due to personal circumstances, I decided to ask for extra hours at work. The main hospital in my area had a job posting for an Exercise Physiologist. I had all the required qualifications and experience.

Proper protocol was to go through my manager to apply as she was responsible for this unit as well as the off-site unit where I was currently employed.

Imagine my utter shock and disbelief when she informed me, that under no circumstances would I ever be going back to work at the main hospital!

She went on to say that "no one there liked me or could stand me."

I couldn't believe these words came out of her mouth.

Was this true? It was not in my realm of understanding. I hadn't any negative experiences with other staff in the main hospital in the thirteen previous years working along side them.

I was very confused. Tears flowed. Old feelings and emotions surfaced. I just wasn't good enough.

This had a major impact on the following three months of my life, my self-esteem, my sense of self-worth, confidence, and belonging.

It took a toll on my physical, mental, and emotional health. It had a detrimental effect on my family life as well as my professional life. I began to question everything, including my skills as a nurse.

Why did I allow her to negatively impose her cruelty upon me? And believe me, I did allow it.

Remember, earlier I said we cannot control the behavior of others? I also said, what was in my control, however, were the choices I made as I navigated the twists and turns that came my way.

Knowing that my choices were in my full control, why would I ever even allow it to enter my mind for a minute, never mind the length of time I did, to give her my power by thinking she was right?

Unfortunately, this wasn't the first time this woman had said things of this sort that were demeaning and degrading. She would often inform me of things that were attacks against my character. Interestingly enough, they had no relevance to my job performance.

Luckily for me, I only had to be in her presence on rare occurrences. It felt to me that she took great pleasure whenever she did meet with me, to ensure that I left feeling damaged.

THERE'S ALWAYS A REASON

I had to face the fact that bullying wasn't new to me. If you recall, I mentioned that I dealt with it as a girl. I have many painful memories associated with being the brunt of meanness.

It was time to go within and get to the root of why.

Why was I so willing to go without? Without confidence, praise, or caring for myself?

Why was I so willing to buy into other people's opinions of me, even when I knew they were wrong?

I knew the time had come and it was up to me to make some changes. Otherwise, I was going to continue going on with life, giving and not receiving, or taking care of my wants and needs.

I had choices to make. Here I was in my forties, sometimes feeling like that "beat-up" little girl.

WEAK KNEED NO MORE!

The time came when I finally woke up and took my power back.

Who was she or anyone else, to think they could continue to bully me (and others) whenever they pleased?

No more! I say enough!

Finally, through sharing my feelings, fears, and concerns, with a counsellor, close friends, and family members, I allowed the walls I had built to crumble.

I found and implemented different practices that would release stress and anxiety.

One of these was laughter yoga. This spoke to me. I practiced it and found the benefits to be amazing! So much so, I am now a facilitator of it. I even use it in my presentations.

Through several healing modalities, I have come to the realization that **I am ENOUGH!**

In fact, I am more than enough.

THE GIFT

Perception is all there is.

As I look back over the events and experiences that have been the culmination of my life, I see things much differently and again, I made a choice. I continue to make strong choices, every day.

I am choosing to acknowledge. I am choosing to receive. I am choosing me.

Now I see that I must, at the very least, fill my cup first, and as it runneth over, I have much to give and share with others, but then and only then.

They may not know it, nor would they likely be pleased about it, but all of the bullies in my life gave me gifts, each in their own unique way.

They pushed me toward learning how to stand up, speak up and show up!

I accept these gifts with grace and gratitude.

Here I am, in all my glory! **I am ENOUGH** and a whole lot more!

AND SO ARE YOU!

Kelly Falardeau is a burn survivor since the age of 2 on 75% of her body. She found a way to go from near death to success, from the ugly scar-faced girl to the TEDx stage, not once but twice.

A documentary about Kelly's life story, **Still Beautiful** launched on TV. In addition, Goalcast launched a video that has over 10 million views.

She is a full-time, award-winning speaker, and Best-Selling Author Strategist, coaching people to become best-selling authors.

Global TV announced Kelly as one of the Most Inspirational People of 2020.

Want to find out how Kelly can help you become a #1 best-selling author?

Feel free to reach out to her at:
www.KellyFalardeau.com
BookKellyToSpeak@gmail.com

WHAT MAKES YOU...YOU?
BY KELLY FALARDEAU

Dreams are meant to be found, not tucked away in Dreamland. ~ Kelly Falardeau

A lot of times I think it's my story of being a burn survivor, getting burned as a two-year-old to most of my body. I used to wonder, why me? Why did I have to go through this?

I remember growing up as a young girl, I would pray to God and I would say, "Dear God, please don't make me wake up in the morning; but if I have to, can I at least be scarless so I can be pretty like all the other girls? Thank you, amen."

Of course, I woke up, and of course the scars were still there. I knew I had a purpose in life. I just didn't know what it was at that point. It took me a while to really discover who I am and why I had to go through what I did.

Looking back through adult eyes, I really believe that I needed to go through getting burned, being bullied, and being shunned, - all of those challenges I've been through. It all helped develop me as a person who is able to teach and help other people to get through their challenges in life.

THE WHY

A lot of people ask me, what is your why?

I've heard a lot of people, when asked the same thing, just say, my why is my kids and family. That's also part of my why, but the real deep why; the why that bring the tears to my eyes, is when someone sent me a picture on Facebook of a little 18-month-old girl who was burned. Her whole body was covered in scars. They said to me, Kelly, she needs one of your blankets (more on these later). I was like oh my gosh, this precious little girl is going to have to go through what I went through. She's going to have to go through all the surgeries. She's going to be teased, she's going to be bullied, and she's going to be shunned.

My why is my kids, but that little eighteen-month-old girl, Rosie, is now seven and I recently just connected with her mom. She has been doing well, at least as well as she can. But she's still going to have to have ongoing surgeries.

That deep passion is what I'm all about because I know, firsthand what it's like to feel like the ugly girl. I know what it's like to know your scars are never going to disappear. I've had so many surgeries to get my scars to disappear and they haven't, but I know I'm beautiful even with my scars.

YES, BEAUTY IS REALLY MORE THAN SKIN DEEP.

It has taken me years and years to discover and understand that beauty is not what you look like on the outside.

Beauty is who we are, how we truly think, feel and act.

With the work I do now, the message I share, I'm often told, "What you guys do is beautiful, connecting charities and non-profits and helping them to do good in the world."

And that is my why; It's my passion.

FEELING UGLY TO FEELING U.G.L.Y.

Let me share a little bit about the backstory of how it all came up. What happened was, I had decided I wanted to do a TEDx talk. The theme of this particular TEDx talk was unprovable or unsolvable problems.

You know how everybody comes up with acronyms? I thought, why couldn't **U.G.L.Y**. be an acronym?

I wanted to prove that **U.G.L.Y**. can actually be a beautiful word.

The 'U' stands for unique because everybody is unique.

I've got a deformed ear and it makes me unique. It makes me special. It makes me different. If we all looked the same, what a boring world it would be.

The 'G' stands for gorgeous, or if you're a guy, good-looking.

We're all gorgeous and we need to stop comparing ourselves to other people.

The L stands for lovable.

The problem with love is that sometimes we don't always see it or feel it or hear it. Sometimes we believe people don't love us, but we are lovable, and we need to reach out to more people and tell them how much we love them, and we will receive it back.

Then of course, the Y stands for you.

The vision I hold is that everybody knows where true beauty comes from and that they're not stuck on having to have surgeries, Botox, or makeup to feel beautiful.

SELF ESTEEM DOESN'T COME IN A BOTTLE

I believe this statement to the core of my being. So much so that I wrote a book called exactly that. *Self Esteem Doesn't Come in a Bottle.*

A lady that I worked for, had a makeup artist come and do my hair and makeup. When I came down after having my hair and makeup done, she said "Oh my gosh are you ever beautiful now!"

I said "Now?"

People think that if I just use certain make-up products, I'm going to be beautiful. They often just don't seem to get it. It's not about the outside, it's about the inner workings. We all need to realize that our true beauty does not come from what we look like on the outside.

She didn't understand it was a trigger for me. I believe I don't need makeup to be beautiful. The impact that I want to have, is for everyone to realize you don't have to wear makeup to be beautiful.

Another impact I want is for everyone to realize, we are beautiful. It doesn't matter if we are overweight or covered in scars!

We are beautiful and I just want to be able to impact all the mothers and daughters, sons, teenagers, and adult men, too.

I think it's all about love and acceptance of who you are.

If you want to make a change, you can, but do it for yourself. Don't do it so that you think somebody else is going to love you. Do it because you need that for yourself.

Let me give you an example, like when I was going to get a new ear.

What they would have done is made a prosthetic ear for me and I would have had to go to the hospital and then I would have had a Snap-On ear. I thought, what if I don't have my ear on and I just have a hole in my head? What are people going to think?

I really got thinking about why or am I/I am doing this. Is it for me, so I can hear better? Or is it for the benefit of people who are looking at me? I'm more comfortable with myself because to me, I wanted a new ear so I could hear better, and it wasn't going to do that.

TAKING BACK MY POWER

I'll never forget one day I went to a garage sale with my former husband, and this older lady said to me, "They couldn't do better than that?" I'm sure you can imagine that I was very upset, hurt and thinking, oh boy, what am I going to say to her?

What she meant was, why couldn't they do some surgery on you and take your scars away? Then you'll be beautiful.

I thought what the heck. She doesn't even know me.

She doesn't know about all the surgeries I endured every two years until I was twenty years old.

She doesn't know about anything I've been through! Eventually, I thought, why am I letting a complete stranger take my power away?

My passion is to do the work I do because I don't want strangers to take power away from people just by making a comment or by looking at them. We're so quick to judge when people look at us.

I remember walking back to my car from a bar, years ago, and one of my good friends from high school was with me. There was a guy coming toward us and he was staring at me. I felt annoyed that he was staring at me, and said to my friend, "I am so annoyed, he's staring at me!"

My friend said, "Kelly, he's staring at you because you're so darn cute!"

But that was the thing. I was always making assumptions, that every time somebody looks at me, they were thinking something negative about me.

It's my passion to help people realize that what other people think is none of their business.

Twelve years ago, I finally accepted my mission in life - to become a public speaker and share my story.

I've traveled all over the world, sharing messages of how we need to love ourselves the way we are and that it's ok to be imperfect. We don't have to be perfect and flawless to be beautiful and loved.

I became a seven-time bestselling author and even traveled to Africa to help burn survivors there. My book is being used to teach self-esteem to girls in the slums.

When COVID hit, I lost all my speaking gigs, and I had no clue what my future would look like. I was a single mom with three teenage kids. I thought, how am I going to support my three kids with no child support, no husband, and now no income?

When I heard the media say we would be locked in our houses and not be able to leave for an indefinite time, I was shocked.

I took my last $500 and went to the grocery store to stock up on food and other supplies. I felt like a zombie watching people load up boxes of toilet paper and cleaning supplies.

Full of fear, anxiety, and hopelessness, I laid on the couch for a week wondering what our lives would look like and thinking about what to do next. I wondered how long it would last and would we survive?

My sister reached out to me and said not to worry, they would help us if we needed money or anything else. We'll help each other like the family we are.

That whole week when I lost all my speaking gigs, I saw my business crumble down to nothing. Then I asked myself this one question "What else can I do, I'm a smart cookie?"

I heard that little voice say, "You're going to do that book thing."

I then thought, how am I going to do that book thing, what's the next step? How am I going to get started?

I saw a post on Facebook that Tad Hargraves was putting on a marketing course and it was 'pay what you can' and learn how to market your small business.

I paid what I could and took his course. After completing it, I thought, instead of reinventing the wheel, why don't I do what Tad did. Why don't I put on a one-day course and teach people how to write their book in seven easy steps?

Because COVID had started, I didn't know if people would have money to pay me so I thought, I can do what Tad did and make it 'pay what you can'.

I was pleasantly surprised. I made $1000 in that one-day course. That's when I thought, let's do this again. From there, I kept doing more workshops and teaching even more people.

I decided to go full-time into coaching people to write their books and become bestselling authors. I hired two coaches to help me take my business to the next level in the digital space and as a result, had my best years ever, financially.

It has been so much fun watching my clients follow my system and become successful bestselling authors. So far, I've helped over 400 people hit the bestselling list, and I have a **100% success rate**.

I'm so proud of my clients. And of me, too!

It's all just so darn beautiful!

Ric Matkowski is a commercial photographer and a digital artist, hailing from a small prairie town in the Province of Saskatchewan. He now resides with his wife in Calgary, Alberta, Canada. He is a multi-accredited photographer with the Professional Photographers of Canada. In addition to his photographic work, his digital art has been featured in multiple publications.

Ric's commercial photography work has received certification from and been recognized by Photigy.com based in Los Angeles, California. Most recently, he was invited to submit his digital art for consideration by Team Canada and their entry into the 2023 World Photographic Cup.

When he is not behind the camera or in front of the computer editing photos or creating digital art, Ric spends his free time reading, and watching a good documentary or action movie. As an admitted sports fanatic, he feeds his addiction to football and hockey by watching as many Saskatchewan Roughriders and Edmonton Oilers games as he can.

Keep in touch with Ric via:
Website: https://www.imagesbyric.com
LinkedIn: https://www.linkedin.com/in/imagesbyric/
Instagram:
https://www.instagram.com/images.by.ric/
Facebook: https://www.facebook.com/RicMatkowskiP
hotography

BOUNCE BACK IN LIVING COLOUR
BY RIC MATKOWSKI

I don't harp on the negative because if you do, then there's no progression. There's no forward movement. You got to always look on the bright side of things, and we are in control. Like, you have control over the choices you make.
~Taraji P. Henson

In 2012, my wife and I decided that it was time to relinquish our expatriate lifestyle, to leave Egypt and move back home to good old Canada. Time had passed quickly! A plan to go and work overseas in 1984 for only a couple of years, turned into nearly 30 years and three kids later!

As an engineer with a large international oil and gas company, the opportunity to work and live abroad was enticing and rewarding. Yes, the money was good as well. We enjoyed a wondrous life, experiencing different cultures and traveling through something like 47 countries and 5 continents.

Our kids all graduated from high school in front of the pyramids and were now back in Canada where they chose to go for their post-secondary education. We were empty nesters!

Along the way, I continued to earn excellent money. We invested the majority of it, and with the 'sack full', it was time to come home, leaving the corporate world behind.

We decided that Calgary, Alberta, was the right place for us. It is a reasonably large city, has an international airport, and while closer to family, not 'too close'. Living there would give us the opportunity to continue traveling while still being near our kids.

These were exciting times. We had much to look forward to as we settled into a temporary accommodation and waited for our international shipment of household effects to arrive.

Next step, find a house that we would call home for the next few years. This task, as we soon discovered, became more of an effort than we first anticipated. Our goal, find an upscale condo where we wouldn't have to spend time with yard work or shoveling snow. Neither of us had any interest in that. It was Canada after all, and it does snow in the winter!

After looking at a number of places, we settled on a new-build in a beautiful, new, upscale development on the south side of the city. The time came to arrange for the transfer of funds. We knew we had more than enough to purchase without a mortgage.

Or did we?

During our time abroad and in particular, the last 8 years, we had made a major decision to invest our hard-earned income with an investment house, owned and managed by Joe, an Englishman, with a Turkish wife.

The firm was headquartered in Istanbul, Turkey. Our relationship with Joe had gone on for 8 years, who had reported excellent returns. Actually, better than excellent!

With encouragingly, strong investment returns, we liberally enjoyed continuing to travel, experiencing several exotic locations. We splurged on the best of resort hotels, meals, excursions and pretty much anything else we wanted.

Furthermore, Joe invited us, and we graciously accepted and participated in unique adventures to Thailand, Formula 1 races in Istanbul, and spectacular gala events in London, England. We'd become good friends with Joe, his wife, and all the staff.

Things are often somewhat more tumultuous throughout various countries in the Middle East than they are in North America. This happened to be the situation we found ourselves in for a short period of time during 2011.

There was a civil uprising in Cairo. Being foreigners, we elected to leave Egypt until it subsided. We were so appreciative that Joe and his team were most accommodating to meet our needs. They organized a fully furnished flat for us, in Istanbul, with a panoramic view of the Bosphorus Strait, complete with shopping and world-class restaurants. Many others who were also displaced at that time, were forced to stay in hotels.

This relationship indeed had all the makings and appearances of being as solid as any!

Or was it?

CHANGES ARE AFOOT

It is now late 2012, and unbeknownst to us at the time, we were about to face some major changes that would affect several areas of our lives.

Our gut instinct, in my opinion, rarely, if ever, fails us. I had a feeling that something was very wrong when I started requesting the cash investment withdrawals that would fund the purchase of our new home. Not only were they were slow in coming, I wasn't receiving the amounts I asked for.

What was going on with our money? Something seems very odd.

Fortunately, with strong effort and much persistence, we were able to withdraw enough to make the purchase and move in. Whew!

As time went on, additional red flags started popping up.

Throughout the course of the next couple of years, still being concerned that something fishy was happening, I requested further and considerably larger withdrawals. My account would indicate that the transaction was being processed.

Imagine my surprise when no transfers were made!

Communication became very one-sided – me to Joe, who all of a sudden was incommunicado.

Finally, in 2014, on what would have otherwise been a normal day, we received the most devastating email! Joe came clean and reported that not only had he been hiding losses, but that he had been issuing bogus reports. The firm was done!

There was no money left and he was closing the doors. Holy sh*t!!!

Talk about a punch to the gut!

My first reaction was total disbelief. I must have read that email a hundred times, checking that it was legit and truly from the investment firm. Confirmed, it felt as if my guts had been ripped out, tossed on the floor, and stomped on. My heart felt like a huge rock plunging off a cliff.

Immediately, I began thinking of the repercussions and how the vision we held for our golden years had immediately vanished.

Massive anger followed. I was ready to reach out and strangle someone, namely Joe.

I just couldn't believe that this person who had become such a big part of our lives, who had helped us during the 2011 Cairo uprisings, had entertained us on numerous trips to Istanbul, had come to Cairo, had dinner in our home and attended our kids' graduations in front of the pyramids, had done this!

Disbelief and anger were immediately followed by total despair.

This was a game-changer!

A DAY-TIME NIGHT-MARE!

To say that I came close to tears on several occasions would be an understatement. I broke down and sobbed, more than once. In fact, now and then the emotions rise up again, and the tears flow.

How could this happen? And why to us?

This was the story you read about in the papers...it just can't happen to me, to us.

But it did!

Certainly, there was a period when a number of investors gathered online, trying to determine exactly what had happened. Also, the big question was, were there any funds to be recovered and returned?

Another painful period followed as I learned of many others who had lost so much, not only their cash but with it, their dreams.

As time went on, a formal fraud investigation was conducted by the UK Anti-Fraud authorities since most of the investors were UK based. They found it difficult dealing with Joe, obtaining records from the investment firm, different authorities, and the Turkish banks.

Wouldn't you expect that for a case of this size, Government authorities would find a way to work together and deliver justice to those so severely harmed? Regrettably, this proved no easy task, and ultimately only minimal records were obtained.

However, luck smiled slightly upon us, and Joe returned to the UK to speak with his lawyers. Was this by design or was it his undoing?

While there he was detained and placed under house arrest, to await trial. It took over a year for the court case to be heard and indeed, Joe was sentenced to three and a half years of imprisonment.

Hardly enough considering how his greed and fraudulent undertakings, had egregiously hurt so many.

I have since heard that his health has deteriorated. I suspect he'll be released early. Perhaps he is out already.

MOVING FORWARD

Everything has its purpose, and this experience is no exception.

As I evaluated my situation, I recognized that as painful as this experience was, I still had a wonderful life...a fantastic family, a wonderful home, and good health. **I have much to be grateful for.**

With that realization in mind, I made a decision.

It was time to try and move on. No, correction. Not try, just move forward.

I considered getting back into the energy business and made some enquiries. I interviewed with one firm, sent out letters and emails to others. In hindsight, these were halfhearted attempts.

Why?

Because deep down I knew I wanted to pursue photography, a spark that was born in my childhood. It was time to give life to this life-long interest.

Certainly, in our time overseas I had taken a lot of photos. You know, the typical family type of shots, most of which were poorly composed, blurry, and generally quite terrible? While still overseas and just prior to our return, I enrolled in some online courses to help improve my skills.

So now, as I sat in Calgary, I decided that the time came time to actively begin.

It started with self-study, spending hours online, watching YouTube clips, reading, taking notes and learning. I can't begin to count the number of hours spent online but I do know it is well over 3000!

Additionally, I started looking at composite photography, a technique of building unique images using elements of many other photographs. This further increased my study time, learning Photoshop, the most popular software used in this type of artistic endeavor. I also looked locally for other ways of improving my photography and joined a local camera club.

Then, as my skills and quality of photographs improved, I became a member of the Professional Photographers of Canada (PPOC) and became accredited in several genres. I also joined organizations with a sole focus on teaching their members about commercial and product photography.

I also joined a couple of international organizations, dedicated to the learning of photo artistry. Access to extended resources, techniques, and established artists in these groups, helped me to drastically improve my photo artistic, art skills.

I'M SAVED

Now here's the thing - photography and digital artistry saved me!

As bad as I felt in 2014, photography and digital artistry were just what I needed to change course and live again. They provided that new focus in my life and a way to move on. Plus, I learned that by being open to grow, learning and applying my newfound knowledge, I could become a photographic artist!

Who? Me?

I have proof!

Yes, as I've become an accredited member of PPOC, I've been featured on a product photography website and my digital artistry has even been featured in a PPOC publication.

A number of my artistic pieces are regularly chosen and featured in several issues of *"Living the Photo Artistic Life."*

Much to my surprise, I've been invited to teach photography in a local high school. I enjoy this very much, knowing that I'm giving back and helping young adults expand their view. Perhaps someone in one of my classes will become a photographer, sharing their passion with the World? Maybe they will even become famous!

I'm honored to have been invited to submit images that will be considered as part of Team Canada's overall submission for the 2023 World Photographic Cup. **This invitation is like being in the running for the Olympics, in the Photography World!**

In the meantime, I continue to learn how to establish a photography business.

My ultimate vision is to own and operate a large-scale, commercial photography firm, meeting the needs of individuals and businesses, not only in Calgary, but all of Alberta, and beyond.

I'VE MOVED ON

My days are full now.

I've forgiven those that have hurt me.

I've forgiven myself for the mistakes I've made.

I made that list, inclusive of everything I forgave myself for, then threw it away, releasing the angst and welcoming the new possibilities.

I've moved on.

Most of us live with a broken and poor model, one that has us wanting before being and doing.

Simplified, a Have-Be-Do model, one where people often express it as, "If I only had this, then I could be that and do the things I want to do."

I was guilty of subscribing to this faulty mode of existence.

I've come to learn that it's important to **LIVE NOW**. To **BE** the person who **DOES** the things that will let me **HAVE** the things I want.

Just look around at successful people and their success stories. You will see that they exhibit these ways of **BE**ing.

The abundance in life is available to all of us. It exists 100% of the time. We just need to see it, become aligned with the Universe, and let it deliver all that we are deserving of.

There are no limitations other than those we place upon ourselves, created by limiting stories that we are running in our subconscious mind.

We are what we focus on, so focus on positive things, things that support you, things you want to be doing and in turn, those behaviors will deliver all that you want to have in life.

Focusing on negative things, diverts your attention from success, and leaves you trapped in a cycle of despair.

Kept suppressed, negativity can manifest as unbearable stress and for some, illness. It is **DIS-EASE.**

Ultimately, it comes down to our thoughts and recognizing that we are not our thoughts, but the controller of them.

So, I implore you, the reader of my story, to know that the world around you is a reflection of yourself. **To change that reflection, change yourself.**

BE the person who **DOES** the things that will deliver what you want to **HAVE.**

And...**LIVE in constant gratitude.**

LaDonna McAbee is a #1 international best-selling author in the anthology, *Cinderella Monologues*, and founder, CEO, owner, entrepreneur, ecommerce e-tailer at Home Sweet Home Treasures, specializing in vintage, retro, new and used, and many custom-made items, Saving the earth one landfill at a time.

Ask LaDonna about the Purposeful Shopping Ambassador Program for your next fundraiser!

Speaker, teacher, domestic goddess of the McAbee clan, wife to her high school sweetheart. 2 Beautiful Daughters + 4 Perfect Grands + Fur Friends = Love Family

In addition to all of the above, LaDonna hosts two livestream broadcasts, **Monday Mojo** and **Throwback Thursday**. You can find them on several social platforms. She would love to have you join her!

Contact LaDonna:
Website: homesweethometreasures.net
Email: homesweethometreasures@gmail.com
LinkedIn: linkedin.com/in/homesweethometreasures
Facebook: facebook.com/HomeSweetHomeTreasures1
Twitter: twitter.com/hshtreasures
Instagram: instagram.com/homesweethometreasures
TikTok: tiktok.com/@homesweethometreasures_1

GOD IS A VERY FUNNY MAN
BY LADONNA MCABEE

Be kind to one another, be kind to our children and nurture them along the way! ~ LaDonna McAbee

God can be a very funny man.

My husband and I had a plan. Our daughters would go to school, graduate, go to college, meet the perfect prince, get married, and have a family.

Isn't that how the fairy tales describe life?

I always said that I would retire when my first grandbaby was born. I also thought I would have wrinkles, gray hair and be financially ready.

When your children experience major changes in their own lives, it affects and changes the entire family, not just the one person.

Turns out, my plan wasn't God's plan. He certainly showed me who was boss!

OUR 18-YEAR-OLD DAUGHTER'S BIG NEWS

My oldest daughter who was still living at home, working and a freshman in college, walked into my home office, on a Super Bowl Sunday. I raised my head up and looked at her. She started to tear up and said, "Mom I have something to tell you. I'm sorry, Mom, I'm pregnant. Please tell dad. Tell him I'm sorry."

She started to sob.

I need to tell you, I'm the kind of Mom who, when necessary, can make an immediate positive thought shift, when it is a benefit for my children.

I then switched into concerned Grandma mode and said, "Stop. Stop crying! It's not about you right now, that baby feels everything that you feel. Don't make the baby sad. Go on to work and please come home when your shift is over. We will figure everything out when you come home. You're not alone! I love you. "

As always, my family comes together and figures it out. No matter what happens we work through it, together. We always have a Plan A and B.

THE DECISION WE ALL HAVE TO LIVE WITH

When my husband came home from work early to watch the Super Bowl, I very carefully gave him the news.

He is a wonderful person, husband, and father. However, as many fathers might likely be, when faced with something this monumental regarding one of his children, he didn't hesitate to loudly express his anger, fear, and disappointment.

Having been married to this man for twenty-one years by this time, of course, I knew him and his immediate reactions very well. Knowing he wouldn't be reacting in his quiet voice, I made sure to send our youngest daughter over to a friend's house until I was confident it was a good time for her to come home.

She arrived home; we sat down to discuss the surprise news. We wanted to ensure that she understood she was every bit as important as her sister and that this would affect the entire family.

It was at this point, we learned that the girls had already talked so she was less shocked than we but had been concerned about how we were going to take the news. We, three, agreed that we would support her sister in making her decisions for the baby. We are family and we do for and take care of each other.

When our pregnant daughter came home from work, we had a family meeting. It went like this:

First, we love you.

There are choices to must be made.

Whatever choices you make will change your life forever.

We talked about aborting the baby. No.

We talked about us adopting the baby. No.

She wanted to have the baby and be a "mommy."

The decision was made that she would have and raise the baby.

We talked about the changes that would have to be made when having a baby.

Growing up with a child, will be different than the carefree life that she had been living.

She would have to become more responsible with her time, money, and patience.

She would now be financially supporting and making decisions for another human.

Sacrifices had to be considered and made.

PLAN OF ACTION

Then it all began.

The plan of action was put in place: doctor's appointments, prenatal care, bloodwork, and everything else that needed to be done when preparing for a baby's arrival.

There are a lot of moving parts and while it may seem that nine months is a long time, the truth of it is, that it is actually a short amount of time to get it all together.

I'm very proud of our youngest daughter. She just hung right in there with us. She supported her sister and helped her with every step that she took.

Watching our young teen daughter navigate through these monumental life changes wasn't all easy. As parents, we were young and doing our best.

It became stressful at times. The decisions that she made affected the entire family, not just her.

While we love our family unconditionally, it doesn't mean there aren't challenges along the way.

During this event our family faced many obstacles. My husband was heartbroken. He always had her on a pedestal. Don't get me wrong, he was there for every need she had before, during, and after the pregnancy.

Because of his pain, he didn't talk to her for the first four months except when she needed him. I had to caution him to keep his words as kind as he possibly could during this time.

Words can be so mean and harmful, and meanness wasn't going to do anyone good. It became a rough time for him, but he needed to keep his emotions in check for our daughter and her baby. He did get better after the first four months. I guess it took him time to get over the shock.

IT'S KINDA SCARY

Our daughter now had to grow up much faster than we would have hoped. She had to think and make decisions for herself and her baby in a new and for her, somewhat scary way.

We knew the importance of being there for her. Through all the hormonal changes, morning sickness, and her body adjusting, There were the mood swings, eating for two, her keeping fit and healthy, along with making sure she was getting to her doctor appointments.

It was time for me to go in for a checkup at the doctors. I felt I should let her know what was going on and WOW, I was blown away with what she had to say. "Congratulations, she is at the best age to have a baby. She is physically fit, and her body is at the best age to carry and give birth. No judgement!" Her response and reassurance lifted my spirits tremendously!

We were all changing mentally and emotionally. Our minds were reaching full capacity as we learned how to handle these changes, while trying to make it a happy, healthy experience, not only for our expectant daughter, but all of us, including our unborn, soon to be here, grandchild.

WHERE'S THE BEEF?

A healthy woman has the best chance to have a healthy, well-nourished baby when she eats good food. This often means they will crave things they don't usually eat.

This baby was craving beef!

Our daughter hadn't eaten beef in four years, but she wanted baby to have what baby wanted and needed. She gave in and started eating beef again.

She was doing everything she could to support birthing a healthy child. Unfortunately, the prenatal vitamins would make her sick. We had to make sure she was supplementing nutritionally in place of them, so she ate what she felt the baby and her body needed to do just that.

THE BIG REVEAL

We all went in together for the ultrasound. We were very excited to see what gender God was surprising us with. And surprise us He did!

A baby boy! What the heck are we going to do with a baby boy?

God is a very funny man!

We raised two girls and had no idea about a boy. I knew that God was looking down, laughing, and saying "You may have a plan, but my plan rules! You may not understand me today, but I know what you need, so hang on for the ride!"

Our minds were spinning with joy that baby and mommy were healthy. An infant male was joining our young, little family of four, soon to be five.

We could hardly wait to meet our new family member.

SHOWER OF LOVE

As we continued to ready ourselves and household for the new arrival, and as is customary where we live, a baby shower was held.

Here was our extremely young, mommy-to-be, glowing and happy, the occasion being joyously filled with supporting family, friends, gifts, and much laughter. The room overflowed with happiness. Those who had borne children of their own, lovingly shared their wisdom for the raising of a child.

She received many gifts that she gratefully accepted and appreciated. It was all about getting everything together for her son's arrival and all these items helped her very much. Her sister never left her side.

Our lovely daughter blossomed into a young woman. It was beautiful to witness.

The nursery and our daughter's room are ready for the new baby.

WHEN IT'S TIME...

Every doctor's appointment went perfectly. Finally, the day arrived when the doctor told our daughter that if she didn't have the baby by early evening on Sunday, she was to be at the hospital at 8pm. It's time for baby to enter the world.

Again, another plan.

We decided that Sunday's dinner would be dinner for four, as we knew it, for the last time. We made a grocery list of what the mommy-to-be wanted, and while she headed to the grocery store to get what we needed, I finished up doing a few things before we headed to the hospital.

Shortly after she left, we received a call from her. **"MOM, I'M AT THE STORE. I WET MY PANTS!"**

With excited laughter, I told her that her water had broken; leave the groceries, go to your car, wait, and I would be there in a few minutes.

Once again, I looked up and said, "God can be a very funny man." We thought we had a plan!

I grabbed her packed bag and her sister drove me to the store where she nervously waited in her car. I drove us straight to the hospital.

Our youngest daughter would also head to the hospital right after calling her dad to let him know the news. He left work to meet us there.

READY OR NOT, HERE I COME

Baby is ready to meet his family and begin his life on the outside!

As with most expectant mothers who carry to term, our young, pregnant daughter was ready to deliver this child.

As you might well know, childbirth is not for the faint of heart. It is painful and this new mom-to-be wasn't interested in enduring more than necessary.

Oh, the wonder of modern medicine! They gave her an epidural, but it didn't work! They gave her another, but it wore off too quickly.

Too late! Baby was ready to make his debut.

Newborns are supposed to let you know they've arrived with a hearty cry, but he wasn't crying or breathing.

This was a terrifying moment. The cord was wrapped around his neck.

Instantly, I dropped to my knees, praying to God to please, let him take his initial breath and let out a loud, "I AM HERE" cry.

Finally, baby began to breathe. We heard him cry. That was the best sound we could have ever heard at that moment. We all took a collective breath and grinned from ear to ear.

I went out to let the new grandpa know that baby was breathing but had to go to the Neonatal Intensive Care Unit. The medical team needed to run some tests to ensure he was going to be okay.

Thankfully, grandpa could go with them, and I could stay with the new mommy.

We waited with bated breath. Finally, grandpa and nurses appear with our new baby. When they put our newborn in his mother's arms, we all freely shed tears of relief and pure joy!

SO MUCH NOISE

As with most newborns, Seth loved to cry, and almost always needed attention, Like all dependent little beings, he was a full-time job.

His mommy was going to school and working. To try and make things easy for us all, I decided to work from home. Do you have any idea how challenging it can be to work with a fussy baby, at times?

It was around this time when my husband showed his ugly side again. It was aimed towards me because he felt I was spending too much time with Seth. His words were mean. I looked up at him and said "Don't make me choose between you and Seth. Like it or not we are in this together, forever."

Someone was jealous!

Not sure what he expected.

Our new bundle of joy never wanted to sleep! Mommy would come home from work and pace the floor. Sometimes, she would drive him around the neighborhood. We did whatever it took, to get him to sleep.

When his aunt came home from school, she would enthusiastically run in to get him, so I could have a break.

Our new little guy was a family affair for sure!

GROWING UP IS SO MUCH FUN

This wonderful boy was my sidekick during the day. He became my shadow and filled my heart with butterflies. The day he first called me Mamaw, was like a holiday filled with laughter and joy! My heart was so full of love, I thought it might spontaneously burst!

I didn't know that I needed you Seth, but God knew.

Seth, you have taught me more than you may ever realize.

Things like, to slow down my life and enjoy the little things, to embrace those special moments.

We are so blessed! That once tiny, baby boy who changed our lives forever is now tall, full of strength, wit, and wisdom.

Seventeen years, and he still fills my heart with butterflies.

He still makes his Mamaw smile and laugh; with her heart so filled with love, she still thinks it could burst!

He will always be our Seth. Yes, he still needs attention, and his whole family love each moment that we get to share with him at this age.

For the young families who may be having an unexpected baby, this may not be your plan, it may not be the right year, day, or moment.

I encourage you to remember that whatever decision you make, you get to live with it forever.

Keep showing and sharing the love you have for each other.

Life isn't always about your plan. God has his plan. He knows what we need even when we don't. You may not understand at the time, but God knows.

Hang on for the ride!

Lois Warnock, Soul Divinity Healing & Art

Spiritual Psychic Artist & Medium; Spirit Coach Strategist

Multi-Modality Energy & Crystal Healing Practitioner

Intuitive Art Instructor

Following a 30-year business career, Lois chose to pursue the 'energy healing' field in 2005, after developing a debilitating chronic condition. She obtained several Reiki Master 'designations (Usui-Angelic-Spiritual), Crystal Resonance Therapy Certification™, Advanced Meditative studies in Primus Healing Techniques™ and Advanced Angel Empowerment Practitioner Certification.

These teachings provided an incredible vibrational healing for her.

During her life she has experienced several near-death-experiences; domestic violence; breast cancer; severe life-threatening infections and a 20-year chronic lung condition. It was in 2012 on a spiritual trek to Alaska, that she was introduced to the Spiritualist teachings, and met her Master Teacher. This was the beginning of her 'soul mission' of spiritual psychic art.

Lois has drawn and channeled over 1,000 spirits for clients around the globe. From this, Lois created the first Spirit Guide Soul Divination Oracle card deck. Lois also offers 1:1 and group coaching programs; individual Spirit Guide Drawing/Readings and paintings.

She will continue to share her story of overcoming adversity, her spiritual discipline and provide you with tools for your spiritual journey.

Lois is currently writing her book, **Oops I'm In The Wrong Body!... A Journey To Embrace Your Divine Soul,** where she shares her story of overcoming adversity by connecting to one's spiritual guides.

Lois's contact info for card deck purchase, website and social media can be found at:

https://linktr.ee/loiswarnock
Email: loiswarnock11@gmail.com

FRANTIC TO BREATHE
BY LOIS WARNOCK

Never say never. ~ Originally from Charles Dickens

My lungs filled with the icy water of the lake as I gasped for air and fruitlessly attempted to hold onto the log spinning furiously out of my desperate grasp. Apparently, choosing the log as a flotation device was not such a good idea!

Unfortunately, the undercurrent kept drifting pulling me out further and further, into the middle of the lake. I can't swim! I heard the scream in my head! All I could do is kick as hard as I could to try to stop from sinking into the depths of the deep lake.

In the distance, I heard other kids playing on the shore along with the adults enjoying a company picnic! I cannot call for help. My dad warned me to stay close to shore because I could not swim yet. He would be angry. As I sink into the icy water for the third time, I feel a strong hand pulling me up allowing my head to stay above the water! A teenage boy has swum out to save me!

Even at the early age of six or seven, I remember I thought *I am going to drown, and no one will notice.* Then, in the next instant, I remember, I was overcome with a calmness in the assurance that Jesus was there - he knows. I not only felt the presence of spirit, I saw it. Was this my first vision?

Years later, I am reminded by my sister, that it was my older brother that saved me, not a neighbor boy as I held in my mind all those years.

As I connect the dots along life's path, I realize that the association of the fear of my dad's anger at me not being obedient, led to this being a major contributor as to why I became so independent, resulting in a 'I can do it myself' attitude, and not asking for help along the way.

THE DISCONNECT CONTINUES

Have you ever felt displaced?

Have you ever felt disconnected from your physical body? You want to feel connected, it's just that your mind doesn't make the connection to who you are or what you are doing? Maybe you do not even understand the disconnect?

I grew up in a remarkably busy and often noisy home with musical instruments playing at any given time; piano, guitar, saxophone, and violin, to name a few. I always called myself the "very middle child" because I was number 6 of 10, that included my five sisters and four brothers.

I was not interested in learning to play a musical instrument, but I loved to dance. I followed that passion, starting with ballet at the age of eight, which led to learning and teaching a variety of styles into my early twenties. Dance helped me to connect to my body more but did not resolve the feeling I still had of being in the wrong body.

I had often thought 'why do I have 'this' body?' even though it was a perfectly good body. I could never explain it to anyone or even describe it to myself where these thoughts even came from. I have memories from somewhere around 6 years old of saying to my mom, "I think I'm in the wrong family. I don't think I'm supposed to be in this family!" She would pat my head gently, trying to reassure me I indeed was in the right place, and then shoosh me out the door, dismissing my concerns, "Okay now go out and play." And life went on.

Over the years, I was challenged by my physical body with typical childhood illnesses of chickenpox and tonsilitis infections. In addition, I suffered severe, debilitating migraines. They were the worst, leaving me in bed for several days at a time – in the dark with hot or cold cloths to alleviate the excruciating pain, the vomiting, and the feeling of being so alone. Again, I wondered why I was in this body. Why? Why? Why? The question played as a continuous loop in my head. What was the point of this?

Many years later, after I started my true spiritual journey, the migraines subsided. Seriously, at the age of fifty-seven or so, it was like one day, just out of the blue, I stopped and realized I had not experienced a migraine for several months.

Interesting that this was shortly after I had begun my spiritual psychic art journey.

Today, in my late sixties, I have connected many more dots.

I have experienced domestic violence; severe lung issues for twenty years, which continued to leave me questioning if I would wake up each morning. Other near-death situations, a serious car accident in which I totaled my vehicle and walked away unscathed, severe leg infections that included a poisonous spider bite during a trip to Arizona that had me walking down the proverbial 'tunnel' with the angels and all my family in spirit.

Oh, did I mention I was diagnosed with Stage 3 Metastatic breast cancer?

In 2000 as I was on the verge of shifting from my government job to become a motivational speaker, the Divine had other plans for me. I suffered a severe, chronic bout of bronchitis and pneumonia. It left me with a constant shortness of breath and coughing spells.

I DEFINITELY FELT, I WAS IN THE WRONG BODY!

For four years, I saw 22 specialists of every kind, with absolutely no definite diagnosis or determining why my lungs and body would NOT heal.

At that point, while I was taking a business class, a colleague who was opening a holistic healing centre, suggested to me 'why don't you take Reiki to see if you can teach that body of yours how to heal itself?' Well, I always said I would try anything – so now I thought – what can it hurt?

That conversation began my introduction into my energy healing journey. It ignited the intense yearning to learn as much as possible on the relationship of energy and its' connection to the physical body.

At some point, we all experience grief through losing loved ones. My family certainly has had their share, as many of those we loved crossed into spirit. They include my dear friend's 17-year-old daughter, several nephews ranging in age from 3 to 42, an older sister, older brother, sister-in-law, brothers-in-law, my mother, my father, grandparents, my mother-in-law, a teenaged grandson, daughter-in-law, aunts, uncles, cousins and many more.

Some of these experiences have broadened my knowledge and connection with the spiritual realm, providing me with a knowingness that while they may no longer be in the physical, they are still close at hand, just in a different form. This is of great comfort to me, especially when family loved ones appear in a psychic art portrait, not just for me, but for many clients.

Over the years, I challenged myself to constantly learn several modalities of energy healing, starting with Reiki. I've done a multitude of meditative studies, spiritual energy work, including psychic development, and crystal resonance therapy. These all facilitated a continued healing of myself. I have had an amazing journey that truly saved my life! I am a life-long learner.

While studying and completing the many certifications I chose, I switched from my full-time business job to being a consultant. My body forced me to make this change to provide flexibility in my life and allow time for my body to heal.

FROM BUREAUCRACY TO PSYCHIC ARTIST

It might well surprise you to learn that for thirty years I worked in positions such as a "government agent" and as a manager of not-for-profit organizations. Add to that, my experience in the banking industry and social services departments. There was absolutely zero correlation between my day jobs and what was to ensue in the very near future.

In 2012, a colleague friend of mine decided to take a group to Alaska for a spiritual trek! **I JUST KNEW I HAD TO GO!** I did not know why but felt such an overwhelming pull toward attending this event, I was determined to make it work regardless of obstacles seemingly in my way.

It was on that journey, as I sat in class learning about the spiritualist teachings of the Masters of the Far East, that the Reverend June stood in front of each student introducing them to their 'Band of Seven Spiritual Team'.

On the second day it was my turn. She stood in front of me and said, "Your Master Teacher is Lord Maitreya, and he is here to tell you that you are a spiritual psychic artist." My flippant response was, **'What the heck is a psychic artist and WHY would I want to do that?'**

She said, "You are not listening; this is different."

Not understanding what she meant, I responded with quips about how there are so many artists in the world, and I have not done any art for at least 40 years since attending high school!

AGAIN, she said "STOP! You are not listening. Now be quiet and hear what your Master is telling you." You could have cut the energy in the room with a knife. It was the most profound energy of pure truth I have ever felt.

That was the turning point. **It was my spiritual awakening "a-ha" moment!**

Throughout the two weeks of intense spiritual classes, with some days consisting of 16 hours in learning mode, I became fascinated with the spiritualist teachings! I became thirsty for knowledge. When I returned home, I wondered, so, what am I supposed to do with this new-found information and ability of psychic art?

I knew I had a choice to make. I could either ignore this new, unknown, spiritually guided path now placed before me and just continue with my life as it always had been, OR I could jump in and trust the divine!

I JUMPED IN without knowing the why, how, or what was coming next! I surrendered to allow in the complete trust and faith in the Divine.

TAKING THE LEAP

Where do I begin?

Not knowing what to do first, I called my spiritual coach and asked how do I start? She arranged for me to stay at her place for a couple of days and told me, "Go buy some art supplies. We will do a meditation and ask for guidance." I agreed with trepidation...what am I getting myself into?

Driving out to her place, towards the Rocky Mountains which held a sacred energy for me, I began a conversation, speaking aloud to myself and whomever else might be listening, even though I was physically alone in my car.

"So, Spirit how is this going to work? Who is going to do the drawing? Remember, I have not drawn in over 40 years!"

Suddenly in the clouds I saw this native chief in spirit appear...seemingly clear as day but translucent! Then in a flash he was gone. "Who's that?" I asked. Again, there was the same flash. This happened several times on the drive out. I continued to ponder and asked questions until I arrived at my destination. I still was not clear on the vision.

We settled in to have tea before starting a meditation. It was only minutes later, when I heard a loud, booming voice in my head, "Get your art paper and pencils, we are ready!" Following direction, I started to draw, or should I say, I held the pencil, and the drawing began.

Within a brief period of time, the native spirit guide I had seen in the clouds appeared on my paper! My coach exclaimed, "Oh I know him; he is my native guide!" Further validation was evident through messages for her.

Okay, I get it now!

AND THE JOURNEY BEGAN...

In the early days, Spirit had me prepare my sacred space and then draw a guide daily. I had only done one painting in high school, over forty years ago. Yes, I was creative with sewing and other crafts during those years. My focus had been my active business career and the raising of two children. Taking this leap was extremely scary!

Slowly my spirit guides would allow me to draw them. I would ask, "Can I please see my psychic artist guide?" NO, you are not ready I would hear. "Can I please see my friends' daughter who transitioned?" "NO, you are not ready!"

I drew guides of all sorts, put a date on them along with any information they gave.

I attended psychic markets to offer spirit guide drawings. Spirit instructed which drawings to bring. It never failed, a client would sit down in front of me and instantly spirit would place the outline of the guide in front of the person, validating that was the guide for them. I would channel messages and finish the drawing. I even amazed myself!

Months into this practice during a morning meditation, my Psychic Artist Guide, Papa Pierre said, "You are ready, get your supplies." As I began to draw, **the pencil went wild**, scribbling so fast all I could do was hang on to it. The energy in the room was palpable! Within 10 minutes, the drawing was done. It was Papa Pierre.

Having been moved to tears during this experience, I wiped my eyes and said, "Thank you." I heard him say, "I know you don't believe what happens 100%, so continue to trust." Then I heard, "Now pick up another paper, you are not finished."

As I began to draw the same thing happened. The pencil took on a life of its' own scribbling and drawing as I held it. Within minutes there was a drawing of a young girl. Oh my gosh I exclaimed, 'It's Jennifer, my friend's daughter!" She tragically lost her life at 17, ten years before. Now what?

It took me a few weeks to get the courage to email a picture of the drawing to my friend. There was no texting then. Within the hour, my friend phoned me asking, 'Why did you send me a drawing of Jennifer?'

I shared all about my Alaska trip, blurting out the psychic art story. I told her Jennifer had messages for them, so we would travel to visit them the next month.

I would love to go on sharing the session with Jennifer's parents along with the plethora of experiences in drawing spirit for people around the globe, but then I would have to author a book.

Oh wait! I am writing a book! Its' release is planned for 2023!

The title of my book is ***Oops, I Am in The Wrong Body...A Journey to Embrace Your Divine Soul***. Read how a shaman medicine woman connected my soul fragments to my heart energetically, allowing me to discover that I am in the right body after all.

Through trusting and listening to Spirit, discover how life's adverse experiences can W.O.W. each of us!

Amy Standridge is the founder and owner of Oak Song Music Therapy and Consulting Services in San Antonio, TX. She is also the co-founder of Grace Notes Community Choir and has been its musical director since October 2018.

Amy's clinical work focuses on people living with dementia and their care partners. As a Board-Certified Music Therapist (MT-BC) since 2000, Amy holds a Master of Music in music therapy from Colorado State University (2000), and a Master of Music in music and human learning with a choral emphasis, from The University of Texas at Austin (2006).

In addition, Amy is currently a Level 2 graduate student of the Humor Academy of the Association for Applied and Therapeutic Humor (AATH).

Amy is a fun, sought-after speaker, and clinician in her local senior adult community, and believes music and humor are a great combination for all.

Amy would love to hear how you use music in your daily life or in a caregiving relationship.

Find her at:

amy@oaksongmusictherapy.com
https://www.linkedin.com/in/amy-standridge/
https://www.facebook.com/oaksongmt
https://www.youtube.com/amystandridge *(You will find some Grace Notes videos here.)*
Sign up for the Grace Notes Community Singers' newsletter here:
https://mailchi.mp/2665e6291e4e/gracenotescommunitychoir

COME JOIN THE CHOIR!
BY AMY STANDRIDGE

In the end, music lifted our spirits and gave us ways to connect with Glen when words could no longer reach him. ~Kim Campbell, widow of country music legend Glen Campbell

Sitting quietly, she looks up and smiles. Is there a memory there, flickering in the periphery of her tired mind? Has the music created an elegant synapse in her cerebral cortex, bringing her to a place of clarity? Her eyes come alive, twinkling for a moment, and she sighs. No words emerge from her lips, but the glow in her eyes speaks. She remembers. It might not be what we would consider remembering, she doesn't share a memory or a thought, but something in the cells of her being remember. I can see it.

This vignette describes a beautiful, smart, beloved wife and mother I worked with. She was no longer able to have a verbal conversation or take care of herself. Sometimes, though, after I would sing hymns to her, holding her hand or giving her shoulder a squeeze, she would say words like "Blessing," "Mother," and "That's beautiful." Even in the very latest stages of dementia, music drew her out. Music brought her back. Music brought us into one another's lives.

I often tell people, "If you are an older person, someone living with dementia, or love someone living with dementia, San Antonio is where you want to be."

MOM KNOWS BEST

"There is a career called music therapy where you can use music to help people," Mom told me when she called.

Music had always been an important part of my life. Playing the piano got me through some difficult times of loneliness and depression in high school and early college. Because of that, music therapy sounded like a great fit, and I was blessed to live in a city that had a music therapy program.

I started taking classes as soon as I could at Charleston Southern University (CSU) in South Carolina. After a year of full-time study, I transferred from one CSU to another - Colorado State University - as a master's equivalency graduate student in music therapy. After much coursework, practica, an internship, a completed master's degree and successfully passing the board certification exam, I could now say I was a board-certified music therapist (MT-BC)!

My first job in this field began at a wonderful music therapy clinic in Austin, Texas. I was assigned to many different client groups including children with autism, young adults with developmental disabilities, adults who had experienced traumatic brain injury (TBI), and older adults with Parkinson's Disease and dementia.

Realizing how much I enjoyed this newfound occupation; I chose to acquire a second master's degree in music and human learning 2006.

After taking a break to start a family with my husband, we moved to San Antonio, Texas where I started my private practice in 2011.

THE BIG QUESTION

"Would you be willing to be our choir director?"

The idea of a choir for people living with dementia had always fascinated me. Wouldn't that be so cool, I wondered?

Without hesitation, I replied with an emphatic "Yes."

"Do you think we can start in two weeks?"

Say no more, my friend. Jumping in headfirst is my love language. Grace Notes Community Choir was born two weeks later.

I felt nervous. I wasn't a trained choir director. I wondered if I could pull this off! We started with eight members - four people living with dementia and four care partners. Most care partners were spouses, but one was a granddaughter who also brought her toddler daughter.

One of our male singers felt hesitant to attend for the first few weeks. Each week we waited with anticipation to see if he would even get out of the car. When he did come in, he sometimes appeared unhappy, sitting in his chair, frowning.

One rehearsal, our apprehensive singer appeared frustrated, not wanting to participate. I had set an easel with a whiteboard on the platform in order to brainstorm some ideas with the choir. Our youngest singer, age two, found her way to the stage and began crawling back and forth under the easel, exploring. When Frank noticed her, he smiled. I never saw him frown again. She became a permanent member of our group, and so did Frank.

Grace Notes Community Choir is my proudest professional accomplishment and the place where I feel the most myself.

One of our original members, the great-grandmother of the young girl, continues to sing with us to the time of this writing. Bea is a petite, vibrant octogenarian who spent most of her adult life singing with a women's barbershop chorus. She is a born performer, singing beautifully and engaging our audiences with her animated stage presence. Like me, I feel like Bea is the most herself when she is singing with us.

Our singers come from all levels of choir experience, from having no choral experience to over 30 years of experience. The only requirements to join our group are an open heart and a desire to sing! Our purpose is the joy and connection that singing together brings.

SAM AND LEANNE

"Here comes the fun" I think to myself when I see Sam come in with his wife, Leanne. Both silver-haired and playful, Sam and Leanne have been singing with us for three years. Neither had any singing experience before jumping right in to join the choir.

At rehearsals, Sam likes to sit with Sandra rather than with Leanne. Sandra is a volunteer, another octogenarian (a person 80 – 89 years old), with a quick laugh, a sparkle in her eye, and a beautifully clear, soprano voice. She and Sam struck up a fun friendship. Wife Leanne thinks it's great when Sam and Sandra sit together!

"Look, Sam, it's your friend, Sandra," Leanne says when they enter the rehearsal.

Sam settles in next to Sandra, looks at her with his bright blue eyes and says, "Hi there, beautiful, it's good to see you again."

"Oh!" Sandra exclaims, laughing, "It's good to see you, too!"

"This woman right here," he tells me, indicating to Sandra, "she's really something. I mean it."

Sam is great with people. He is the first to shake hands with a new person who comes into the room and is quick to share a kind greeting. I know that Sandra appreciates his encouragement. After a long break from singing with a group, she is overjoyed to sing and perform again. Sam's praise is important to Sandra.

You might think that the person living with dementia is always the one in a position to need encouragement. In this case, he is the person spreading cheer. Sam's personality and natural abilities shine through during our rehearsals. We love him, and he can tell.

Our choir encourages musical "duets," a person living with dementia and their care partner, to sing along with volunteers. Ideally, each singer with dementia would have a volunteer to sing next to them and assist them with whatever they need.

For example, sometimes Sandra helps Sam turn pages or find his place in the music. This gives volunteer Sandra a sense of purpose. This also allows Leanne to choose to sit with friends in the chorus, sit with her choral voice part, or sit with Sam if she likes.

Even the strongest relationships need a break sometimes. Care partners in a dementia relationship might not have that option very often. Not only does the healthy partner need a break, but the person with dementia also needs the chance to build relationships with people other than their partner.

Our need for social interaction does not decrease as a result of having dementia, it increases.

Maintaining a vibrant social life for as long as possible is a great way to combat the isolating effects of dementia diagnosis both for the care partner and the care receiver. Choir rehearsals invigorate social life!

Sam often tears up when he speaks about what our choir means to him. Although his language is sometimes convoluted, his intention is clear. These are good people, I love being with them, and we should never stop meeting. Sam has such a good sense of humor; it is sometimes hard to tell if he is joking. "No, I'm serious," he says, "it means a lot." He's right.

LAUGHTER IS GOOD MEDICINE

We have a spirit of fun in our group. We work hard, learning new music and practicing familiar music, and we laugh a lot at every rehearsal. Sometimes a choir member will share a joke or a funny story, but more often we giggle at each other's one-liners, facial expressions, and even at our mistakes. Especially at our mistakes.

Recently, I printed some lyric sheets for a performance. One of the songs we sing is "Home on the Range." Here's what our lyric sheet said, "Home, home on the range, where the dear and the antelope play. Where seldom is heard a discouraging word, and the clouds are not cloudy all day."

Read that again. Can you find my two errors? Listen, I live in Texas and there is some truth to that statement! But every time we came to the lyric errors, we smiled. Part of me didn't want to fix them because it made us all chuckle inside.

A good laugh does all kinds of amazing things for our bodies and for our relationships!

I always leave choir rehearsals with a deep sense of well-being and contentment. I remember the first year we were together. Each time I left rehearsal I thought to myself, "I can't believe how awesome and fulfilling this is!" I felt extremely blessed to be leading this vivacious and open-hearted group of singers. I thought there was nothing better.

Our choir started receiving some local news coverage and were scheduled to perform at a conference at our local Alzheimer's Association for our second year in a row. We were also preparing to become an official program of our local Meals on Wheels. We were really thriving!

No one could have expected what happened next.

When we started hearing reports of a global pandemic taking our world by surprise, my heart plummeted. I found myself panicking about what would happen to our precious choir. As a result of the world's circumstances, the conference was canceled. Choir rehearsals were suspended indefinitely.

ABOUT, FACE!

At the time, our choir was funded through a grant from a local university. I felt incredibly relieved when it was suggested that we take our choir rehearsals online. Like many others, we found ways to adapt to our unprecedented circumstances. We are resilient! We met online via Zoom for two years.

Remarkably, in all of that time online, we didn't lose a single duet from lack of interest. In fact, we gained several more couples who learned about us during the pandemic. Sam and Leanne chose not to attend "virtual rehearsals," but returned as soon as we resumed live rehearsals.

During the time we met online, we sang, laughed, shared hobbies, and showcased heirlooms from our homes. We even learned that one of our singers is a talented painter! We supported one another during a time of fear and uncertainty.

We became a family.

After two years online, the decision about when to meet in person again seemed daunting. It felt like the minute we would decide it was acceptable to do so, a new setback occurred. We moved forward cautiously.

As a first step back to resuming in-person rehearsals, our accompanist started coming to my house to co-lead rehearsals with me. She and I would lead from my living room, and each of our duets joined from their own homes. Before this point, I accompanied most rehearsals with my guitar. It felt amazing to have a pianist again! We started learning new songs that everyone was excited about, in anticipation of finally singing together again.

What a triumph when we were finally able to sing together face-to-face!

WE'RE BAAAACK!

"So, we'll see everyone next week?" several members asked joyfully at the end of that first in-person rehearsal.

I thought choir members might want to start off singing online every other week. Nope! It suddenly felt like the sun had finally come out and we wanted to leave the blinds open!

Everyone celebrated being together again. This was especially true for Sam and Leanne who re-joined us after our two years online adventure.

At the time of this writing, Grace Notes has been rehearsing in person for almost a year. We have two performances coming up and are officially a program of Meals on Wheels San Antonio.

WHAT'S NEXT?

In the words of a former choir member, "Dementia is a screwy disease." A dementia diagnosis understandably brings fear, anger, sadness, and confusion. And yet, it's not a time to give up. It's a time to engage!

Dance, fresh air, and rides in the country still exist. Community musical events, concerts, and theaters are still available.

Musical experiences offer a sense of normalcy, comfort, and hope. It gives us aesthetic beauty, emotional support and builds bridges when we feel far away. Perhaps you can find a dementia-friendly chorus where you or your loved one lives.

Open your heart to the power of music to wonderfully enhance your life!

Tony Kaufman is a 6x International #1Amazon Bestseller: Author and contributor.

She went from working with Former President George H.W. Bush as his personal computer trainer and support for his offices and homes, to returning to her producer roots in Television, Radio, and Podcast. Co-Founder of The Standout Stars Speakers Bureau, Toni's production/casting background (in English and Spanish) include such famous shows as The Latin Grammys and the Texas Music Awards, as well as Fremantle Media's Top Talent Searching programs and their Spanish Counterparts: American Idol/Objetivo Fama, America's Top Models/Belleza Latina, and casting families for Family Feud/Que Dice La Gente, among many others.

Toni went from owning and managing high-profile corporate teams to creating a network of World Class Mentors that host a multitude of influencers from industries such as oil, technology, speaking, politics, and film/TV. She is dedicated to celebrating those who have achieved world-class by honoring their mentors, their own lives, and legacies.

Toni Kaufman and her business partner Sheridan Wickens Fogg are cohosting the SOS TV show airing on EZWay TV. They are a dynamic speaking duo, who work with entrepreneurs, speakers, authors, healers, and coaches to help them find clarity, revive their message, design sizzling campaigns to increase sales, deliver authority, and bring out their inner hero.

Toni brings a hi-energy level of empowerment to her audiences, from near-death experiences to driven, absolute entrepreneurship. Motivated and inspired are two descriptions of how her audiences leave after her talks.

https://linktr.ee/tonikaufman

THE RING
BY TONI KAUFMAN

A superhero is only ever shown to be as powerful as the villains they conquer.~ Ariel Todd Kaufman

"You've never looked at a person and been totally vulnerable,
Known someone that could level you with their eyes,
Feeling like God put an angel on Earth just for you
Could rescue you from the depths of Hell, and you would know what it's like to be an angel.
To have that love for them, to be there, forever, through anything, through Cancer.
And you would know about sleeping sitting up in a hospital room for two months holding their hand because the doctors could see in your eyes that the terms Visiting Hours don't apply to you.
And you would know about real loss because that only occurs when you
love something more than you love yourself"

Aaptation from Good Will Hunting

As of this very moment, there are people all over the world who are just like you and me—they are lonely, they are missing somebody, they are depressed, they are hurt, they are scarred from the past, they are having personal issues no one knows about, they have secrets.

One of my daily prayers starts like this: "Even when you don't see it, God is working things out for your good. Thank you God for what you have allowed me to experience in my life. The unconditional love of a wonderful father and mother, The strength and love, the laughter of the comedienne that was my big sister, The true love of a man that just took my breath away. The unconditional love that I have for my children and grandchildren and thank you God for the lessons you have delivered to me in my life."

AUGUST 2017 - HURRICANE HARVEY

What nobody knows, except my children, is that after Hurricane Harvey, we had just completed repairing the house from the April Tax Day Flood of 2016. I just could not take 3 more weeks of 20 mitigation drying fans going on round the clock day and night, another round of fire ants, bed bugs and watching the claw pick up everything that I owned from the sidewalk, while the entire family lived in two upstairs bedrooms with a makeshift kitchen in the middle room and a bathtub full of dishes to wash each time we tried to cook anything.

But more than that, I spent 30 years of marriage to a functional alcoholic who spent most nights and all weekends sitting alone in the garage with his music playing until he would drink himself into a diabetic coma, and then we would have to call 911 or pour syrup down his throat to get his blood sugar back up above 27 to save his life. By this time, I had lost so much respect for my husband that I did everything I could to stay away, dedicated myself to my work, launched a new company, immersed myself into studying, learning, and doing everything I could to not feel.

My anger was always there. My failure, guilt, and inability to control what was supposed to be the most important part of my life was going nowhere. I chose to miss weddings and family events because I knew he would get drunk and embarrass me, and I did not want to deal with the humiliation.

I was comfortable. I was miserable. So, I traveled a lot. However, our sons did not. When I left they kept the watch on dad, listening for noises in the night, understanding that if he went into a diabetic coma he could die., So, one of them slept in the same room, stayed in the same house and in the process, gave up his life and girlfriend in order to ensure that dad would wake up the next day.

We all believed that Kirvin's depression and addiction was going to ultimately kill him. I moved out, I found a home that had never been flooded and set up my office in that location, away from the construction and away from everything that I had no control over.

CHRISTMAS EVE, 2017

Kirvin and I were on our way to celebrate at my little brother's home in Tomball Texas., Anthony, was in his second year with a liver transplant and we had just found out that he had Prostate Cancer. Anthony was the one person I could always talk to, he understood, he was my strength, and I was his go-to when he needed. We shared so much, we were the two youngest and we stuck by each other, especially when he got sick.

There we were, in Walmart on Christmas Eve. I was looking for last-minute presents while Kirvin was looking in the jewelry section. I finished my shopping and got back to the counter where Kirvin stood with a box in his hand. "Baby," he said, "would you marry me?"

"Are you crazy?" I asked. "I will not live with a smoking alcoholic, and before you are allowed to move into the new house, you have to clean up."

Keep in mind that our past 30 years were riddled with broken promises of sobriety and quitting smoking, to the kids and me. We were all hurt so many times. "Baby, I'm ready," he said, "let's try this again." After all this time, I was still in love with this man, so just for Christmas and to keep a positive facade in front of the families, I said, "Yes."

It is not a very pretty ring. It does not look expensive. It cost all of what we had at the time, around $500. There is no solitaire on top, rather a cluster of little pieces of diamonds and diamond dust.

2018 - A DIFFERENT SORT OF YEAR

Kirvin had been keeping his promise, started seeing a nutritionist, worked hard trying to keep his diabetes in check. He tried the insulin pump, chewed nicotine gum, and overall started getting really healthy. He never bought beer, did not drink any alcohol.

He was going to the doctor and losing weight. We were so proud of him. But then, he could not stop losing weight. It was changing him in ways that did not make any sense. And then the pain in the right hip started. After a blood test, which included a PSA panel, his readings were at 57, more than 50 points above normal. Kirvin had stage 4 prostate cancer that had metastasized to his bones, spine, and hips.

On January 19, 2020, Kirvin passed away on the second day of our last cruise, onboard the Carnival Magic somewhere over the Caribbean Ocean.

A FITTING TRIBUTE

We were so immensely proud of Kirvin, I just have to share the eulogy written by our sons:

"Hello, for those of you who don't know me, I'm Todd, Kirvin's youngest, and I'd like to tell you a little about him today and paint as clear a picture as I possibly can of a man who often preferred the company of a good book and a radio than most others, escaping into the worlds and realms and possibilities of galaxies far, far away.

While I adored my father, I'd understand if you told me you had complicated feelings about him, I think most people who knew him well might, and it's okay to feel that about frankly a complex man.

In high school and college, I was deep into superhero comics, and despite how audacious and ridiculous their back stories may have gotten, it was always so easy for me to believe them. Why wouldn't I? I had heard my dad's back-story. Kirvin was born in Kwigilingok, Alaska. He was raised in an Inuit Village and then a Hopi Indian reservation. Eventually his family ended up in Austin, TX where the children were separated from their mom after she was confined to the state hospital. He was sent to a series of children's homes until ultimately, he arrived in Mission, TX at the Rio Grande Children's Home. He graduated salutatorian of Sharyland High School, class of 1970.

A brilliant man with an incredible mind and a smile you could spot from across the room, he was nominated to the Air Force Academy and ended up narrowly missing going to Nam because after all his pilot training, he grew, and it does say this on his records, three inches too tall to be a pilot.

Kirvin and Toni married on Easter Sunday, 1987 and moved to Austin with her children, Andrea, and Mikael, then to Houston with their two - James Erik and Ariel Todd.

His work ethic will always be burned into my mind. The first signs we got that he was not doing well was when he started needing to come home early, or not go in at all. That is when you knew something was up, he knew the importance of being on time, of doing a job well, of being a reliable asset to the people around you.

My father was infinitely reliable if it was something he did not mind doing. The sort of security you get from your favorite winter sweater, you knew where he was, you knew what he was probably doing, and you knew he loved you.

Superheroes, of course, have their flaws too. Few people get to see Iron Man's alcoholism. Few people get to see the depression on ink and paper in the small squares of the comic strip.

*There are demons and villains that we all fight on a daily basis, but **I think a superhero is only ever shown to be as powerful as the villains they conquer**, and so it would be remiss of me to try and downplay the havoc that they wreaked.*

I know my own and my siblings memories, even the happier ones, have at the very least, a beer goggle tinge, but I bring this up because I can say, with a shining certainty, that this was a war that my father won. It may have taken years, but for the last few, my father had successfully overcome his alcoholism, even his smoking habit, and he did those before he had been sick. He was getting healthier, and he had a renewed will to live these past few years that, perhaps makes this all just a shocking situation?

But now I would like to take a second to talk about the softness of this superhero. Of a man who, despite the fact that he could not help you with your homework unless you could take some yelling but would let your friends stay over as long as they needed a place. Who taught me the importance of working hard and testing out your theories. Who taught me that it is okay to not take life too seriously and that sometimes it was okay to laugh it off. He wanted to retire and run away with me to the Renaissance festivals I work at and would tell me about his plans to get a manual crank snow cone machine and dress as a monk.

A man who was real with me, but supportive. And who, even when I put him in some particularly tough situations to be in as a father, I would have to say passed with flying colors, even if just in his own quiet way. I will miss going to events with you, Dad, just to leave over an hour early under the guise of 'wanting to beat traffic' and knowing that we'd both just actually rather be at home.

The Kaufman family crest is an imposing field of black with a single silver anchor adorned on the front, and I often think of my father's idle musings of being a sailor. His love of Horatio Hornblower, admiration of giant wood vessels and even coming as a pirate captain to my themed wedding, I have to say that I am at peace knowing he passed while out over something he'd had a lifelong passion for, because I honestly don't know how many of those he may have truly had, and I like to think of him doing now all the things he ever wanted to do. Seeing all that he wanted to see. And at the same time, I feel closer to him now, because I know there is a part of him that is now always the sun on my back, the wind on my face, and my favorite warm winter sweater. The warmth of his love. Thank you."

THE REALITY OF YOU

My ring is perfect. The pieces of the diamond are better than the whole. They represent the pieces of my life, 33 years dedicated to my husband and children, to making this world a little bit better than how I found it, to believing in love and all the happiness it can bring.

You too can be happy anywhere you are, you do not need anyone's approval, you are enough, you are strong. Other people can be part of your journey, but they cannot and never will be the destination. Never put your happiness in another person's hands, it does not work like that, it is more like a state of mind, but you get to make it. Not anyone but you.

You can be happy in a small cottage. You can be happy in a big city, as long as you are a friend to yourself. You are loved and worthy; do not allow others to make you believe otherwise. Only you know yourself well, they see just a picture of you their mind made. But it is not you. Not exactly. You are capable of anything your mind can think of. If it is there - you know it is possible.

You are the center of YOUR universe; you can do anything you want. And yes, you are strong enough to achieve it. You just are. Even if you are scared or insecure, trust me, and trust yourself. You are capable. You set your own goals.

Remember: the point is to be happy. You can never dream too big or too small. Your goal is to be happy, so go, do whatever it takes to achieve it! I believe in you, and I love you. You know it is true.

If you are reading this, regardless of where you are right now on this planet, I wish you a wonderful night, and a happy peaceful life where all your dreams become true.

"Thank you God for what you have allowed me to experience in my life, The unconditional love of a wonderful father and mother, The strength and love, the laughter of the comedienne that was my big sister, The true love of a man that just took my breath away. The unconditional love that I have for my children and stepchildren and thank you God for the lessons you have delivered to me in my life."

Contact Toni at:

https://linktr.ee/tonikaufman

Debora J. Hollick, *The Smash Through Mentor*, is an International Speaker, Intuitive Consultant & Strategist, Trainer, Coach, and 3x International #1 Best Selling Author.

She specializes in motivating pleasant human interactions that optimize powerful work performance and productivity boosts.

Debora helps businesses and professionals ★ smash confusion, ★ solve chaos, and ★ stop cussing, while they are resolving challenges. Her clients say, ***"It feels like, receiving a warm, energy hug while also receiving a gentle kick in the pants!"***

People hire Debora as a Keynote Speaker, to facilitate workshops and events. She is able to speak on several topics, a few of which are:

A Selfie of a Different Sort

Listen to the Whispers or...Get the 2x4!

The Bully Lives Within

She is the founder of **Live Life In W.O.W! Wonder~Openness~Wisdom**, an anthology books, Companion Playbook, and events.

Call it Karma, Good luck, or a Spiritual Intervention...however you want to describe it, you can't help but believe that Debora J. Hollick, *The Smash Through Mentor*, is destined to help people discover a better version of themselves!

If you would like to have Debora share her wisdom with your organization or find out how you can become a contributing Author to her books, please:

Contact Debora:
LinkedIn:
https://www.linkedin.com/in/deborajhollick
Email: Debora@smashthroughmentor.com
Website: https://smashthroughmentor.com/
Facebook
https://www.facebook.com/SmashThroughMentor

JUST... BE A DUCK!
BY DEBORA J. HOLLICK

We often add to our pain and suffering by being overly sensitive, over-reacting to minor things, and sometimes taking things too personally. ~ Dalai Lama

My youngest sibling is funny, witty, and wise. She comes up with the best lines that not only make me laugh, but they are also full of practical and while sometimes odd, great advice. One of those such lines is **"be a duck."**

Are you are wondering what is so great about that? What is so practical and wise in her instruction? A little back story will help.

I can't fully recall exactly what we were discussing, and nor do I want to, but it had something to do with family dynamics. As I'm sure with most, if not all, families from time to time, there are differences of opinion, and hurtful things are said that are just hard to let go of.

So, we stew over them. We analyze and replay the perceived scenarios, over, and over again. Often, past memories and issues arise that we now decide to include for good measure, and we wonder why anyone would say these things to us, especially another family member!

SOUND FAMILIAR? YOU, TOO?

We discussed the situation (she was not the injuring party), and I expressed my thoughts and feelings to her, that I felt confused, sad, hurt, and, more likely than not, a bit angry. She is a very good listener.

It was more than obvious to her that I allowed the remarks to affect me and how I felt about myself. After all, would we not all most likely prefer our family members to like us and treat us kindly? Even if we don't agree or even understand each other's viewpoint?

She knows me very well and understands that I am sensitive. She is a great mediator and always tries to be fair considering all parties concerned. She shares her thoughts wisely, and then manages to lighten the mood while providing sage advice.

ESPECIALLY DURING THE HOLIDAY SEASON AND SPECIAL OCCASIONS!

"Be a duck. Just be a duck," she says. In other words, just let it glide off your back. No need to carry it further.

Fall is coming to a close. As we embark upon festivities of the season, that many celebrate with family and friends, it is important to remember that while some may be full of joy and excitement, others, may be struggling through challenging times.

We live during a time and in societies where, or at least though it seems, so many are choosing the path of being offended by the words and actions of others. While I fully believe and support that everyone is certainly entitled to their feelings and opinions, shaming, and condemning others, just because their feelings, and opinions differ from yours, and what they said or thought, slighted you in some way, isn't, in my opinion, helpful to anyone.

Rest assured, I am not advocating that injustices, discrimination, or cruelty of any sort, is to be tolerated or accepted, what I am referring to are the little things. Things like:

> How someone chooses to decorate their home for the holidays,

> What colour someone chooses to dye their hair or what style they wear it in,

> What style people choose to wear,

> What traditions people celebrate, and so on...

> You get the picture.

Why is considering others such an important act?

Not only is it the kind and respectful thing to do at any time of the year, but it could also have a direct effect on how the person on the other end, perceives their value and worth.

Simply put, it is the right thing to do.

Have you ever felt that someone berated or belittled you in some way, and then you experienced a feeling of unworthiness?

It is important to note that our self-esteem has a great impact on our choices and decisions.

This is true even though they may not have meant to make you feel the way you did.

PERCEPTION IS EVERYTHING

Let us put our best foot and thoughts forward, doing our utmost to cradle with care, the self-esteem of others. Let's endeavor to do this, not only during what may be considered to be one of the happiest times of the year, by some, but always.

Why is it that we tend to be nicer and more considerate on special occasions like birthdays, weddings, and funerals?

I wonder what would happen if the majority decided to treat every day like a special occasion and behave as such?

Just imagine...for a moment...how much easier our own lives would be if we made conscious decisions, as often as possible, to see things in a lighter sense.

Just what if...what if, it made us feel better?

What if each of us developed our **superpower** to choose to see more of the beauty, abundance, and love that truly is everywhere around us and, in every culture, religion and race? I believe we all are capable of this if we want to put forth some effort.

What if, we started to look for the **W.O.W! – the wonder, openness, and wisdom,** in ourselves, each other and the world around us?

And what if, each our small efforts made a difference?

Will we always be successful at it? For most of us, likely not, but any improvement in our behavior toward others will be helpful. And the more often, the better!

One never knows the impact we might have on another human being just by leaving them with a feeling of being seen, heard and whole, regardless of the circumstances.

Put down those heavy burdens. They do not serve you or anyone else in a positive light.

You don't want to drown under the weight of it all, so...

BE A DUCK!

Teresa Brunner hails from a small town in Saskatchewan, Canada and now resides in Edmonton, Alberta, Canada. Her country roots still reside deep within her, and she is always taking the back roads in her travels. You can take the girl out of the country, but not the country out of the girl!

Her mother played an important part in her love of handicrafts by encouraging, teaching, and supporting her journey of sewing, quilting, petit point, needlepoint, knitting, crocheting and more. Her biggest loves though are quilting and making teddy bears from fur coats.

Next year will mark 20 years she has been making teddy bears from recycling fur coats and turning them into treasured heirloom keepsakes. Teddy Bears found Teresa. These teddy bears "speak to her" telling a story with each one she makes. Today she has created approximately 250 bears, and they reside all over the world, from Australia to the high Arctic, Sweden to the east and west coasts of Canada and the United States.

Her clients are so happy and excited with the memories that are evoked every time they pick up their bear and hug them. They are so grateful that Teresa was able to create a legacy encapsulating their precious times, that will continue throughout their families for generations to come, bringing even more memories to life, through her lovingly hand-crafted bears.

Ask Teresa about how you can have your very own unique heirloom keepsake or treasured Memory Bear at:

Website: www.teddymybear.com
Email: teddymybearteresa@gmail.com

DID YOU KNOW THAT TEDDY BEARS REALLY CAN TALK?
BY TERESA BRUNNER

*Long before I grew up my Teddy Bear taught me what love
really meant: being there when you're needed.*
~ Jim Nelson

We, Teddy Bears are so very excited to tell you our story. It is our tale of how we came alive, to be loved and treasured.

It all began during 2000 when our maker, Teresa Brunner, started learning how to make bears. Turns out, she was pretty good at it, and in 2003, after making bears of all sizes, out of many different fabrics, Teresa was inspired to begin making them from old fur coats.

This brought new life to treasured keepsakes by recycling and repurposing them.

You see, women who purchased or were gifted fur coats in the years between 1950 and the 1980's or thereabouts, felt they had "made it!" They had saved up enough money to buy or perhaps someone bought for them, a luxurious fur coat.

At that time, and for many years to follow, fur coats were considered a status symbol. It presented one as a member of an elite class. They were worn by many women from all walks of life, as well as heads of state, the Queen and many famous movie stars and celebrities.

To own and wear one was very much the fashion, that you were important It announced to all that you had "arrived."

Is it any wonder then, that those women who have enjoyed this experience and the memories associated with it, revere and treasure their coats, worn as they, may be? Should it really come as a surprise that they yearn to pass them on to their daughters, granddaughters, nieces, and yes, even sons, grandsons, nephews, and others whom they love and appreciate?

Style and societies change. Unfortunately, for many, most people no longer wear them for fear of having paint sprayed on them by animal activists.

Some coats are made of heavy fur, and people are no longer willing to withstand wearing them for any length of time. Perhaps, they no longer fit physically, or the owner may have changed. For many though, living in harsh, cold climates, there is nothing greater than wearing a fur coat in the winter. They not only block out the wind and keep you toasty warm, but they also cloak you like they are giving you a big loving, bear hug.

Are you wondering how Teresa got into making teddy bears from fur coats, and why she continues to do so to this very day? Let us tell you.

Teresa didn't find Teddy Bears.

We found her!

Yes, you read that right.

We found her!

This may come as a surprise to you, but we had been searching, hoping, and watching for someone special to come along. Someone who would understand what it would mean to the giver and receiver of us. Someone who uses their intuition to create not only our soft, furry bodies, but also our personalities, complete with accessories!

And here she was! Oh my! Our tiny hearts were filled with so much love and joy. Our hearts were going pitter, patter, pitter patter. We thought they might burst with excitement!

As a young girl, Teresa always had some sort of stuffed animal around her in her bedroom. She remembers being tucked into bed with all her animals snuggled in around her, keeping her warm and cozy. So, we knew she was the one!

In 2003 a long-time friend called her up asked, "Teresa, do you know anyone who makes teddy bears from old fur coats?"

Her Mom had recently passed away and she wanted to have teddy bears made from her mom's fur coat. Teresa's response to her was, "Not off the top of my head, but leave it with me for a bit and I'll see what I can find." It was maybe a couple of weeks later, and Teresa received a newsletter in the mail. *Learn How To Make A Teddy Bear From A Fur Coat* was the headline. Hmmmmm... she thought...maybe I should be making teddy bears for my friend! This, surely, is a sign that her mom, whom Teresa knew, was talking with her!

And there you have it. Teresa signed up for the class and ended up making five delightful teddy bears for her friend, from her mother's precious coat. Teresa fell in love with working with fur and decided she wanted to make more of them.

Teresa knew that if she really wanted to do this, she could not make these special bears from the commercial patterns she was buying, so she went about learning how to design teddy bear patterns.

Her own first fur, bear, babies were Nikki, Andy, Sabrina, Wendy, Margaretha, and last, but not least, Sharon. Teresa was able to tweak the patterns, and tweak she did, until she was happy with the final design. What a thrill it was, to have these bears come alive as she added their ears and eyes!

Next, as her journey progressed, was to come up with a name for her newfound business.

Teresa wanted to use her initials which worked out well with Teddy Bears, but what can I use for my middle initial "M", she pondered. Well, what else what there to do but brainstorm with close friends? And so began "***Teddy My Bear***."

Over the course of about the past twenty years, Teresa has had the pleasure of making about 250 treasured, heirloom, keepsakes, for many individuals and their families. It is so exciting to know they reside all over the world.

Now, for the stories that Dorothy, Margaret, and Yolande, told Teresa, as she brought us to life.

DOROTHY

Hi. My name is Dorothy.

The bears have already told you how Teresa's business was created and through it, how she is reviving fond memories for loved ones. In my opinion, it really is all about the memories and creating a legacy for family members.

Why did I wait to die before I gave you something that was a so very important piece of me?

Oh, how I would have loved to see the look in your eyes when you brought the bears home.

Can you feel the love I have for you? Can you feel my arms around you each time you pick up your bear?

Can you see the tears of joy in my eyes? Do you remember seeing me wearing the coat your bear came from. Maybe you were with me when I was wearing it. Is there was a special memory like you always touching and feeling me…after all, my fur coat is ever so nice and soft.

Maybe you saw me stand a little taller and a little prouder when you saw me in the fur coat. I hope so because that is how I felt when I wore it.

Marjorie was a very devoted daughter. When my health was ailing, she came home to take care of me, as I did when my mother, Ella, needed me.

Marjorie refers to her Ella Bear (that is the name she decided upon), that is made from my treasured fur coat, as her "healing bear." When I see her hug it, I get the sense that it is almost like she feels she has again, come home and it is blending generations together.

I know she finds great comfort and healing in Ella Bear's presence. I think that is because she can feel I am still sending out so much love to her and anyone else who sees me on display.

MARGARET

Hi. My name is Margaret, and just to let you know I still speak to Teresa and her friends. This is my story.

My bears were made from the fur coat I had as a young woman. My three children wanted to have bears made from my brown, Persian lamb. My coat was so beautiful. Teresa had never seen a brown Persian lamb before. She thought I would be black, gray, or even cream. She fell in love with my soft brown color.

Imagine her surprise when I was able to get her to squeeze just one more bear from my fur coat!

When she spoke with my daughter, she wasn't 100% sure she wanted four bears and told Teresa she could make up the fourth bear and keep it for herself. Hmmmm...I thought, I need to start talking to Teresa more. I don't think my daughter realizes how important this fourth bear will be for her.

So, as Teresa was finishing off all the bears in my family, she needed to come up with a name for me. Well, Margaret is her middle name, but no this isn't it...I must make sure there is another reason for her to choose Margaret. I need to make sure my daughter will know it's me.

So, I made sure Teresa chose pearls to dress me up. She found me a lovely necklace, even a bracelet, and adorned my ears with some pearls. And, to make absolutely sure my daughter really knew it was me, I had Teresa put the initial "M" on my foot pad!

The day came when Teresa came to meet up with my daughter, who was so excited, she prepared a "teddy bear picnic" to welcome us.

I was about to be brought home and revealed to my daughter!

She fell in love with the first three, just like I knew she would. She couldn't stop touching them and her eyes were always going back to them.

Then, Teresa brought me out. Imagine my daughter's surprise! She said "Teresa, what did you call this bear?"

"Well, I called her Margaret."

"Why did you call her Margaret?"

"Well, I'm not exactly sure, she just felt like a Margaret to me."

"Well why did you dress her up with pearls?"

Teresa's response was, "I'm not sure. She just seemed to call for wearing pearls to me. Why do you ask?"

My daughter answered, "Well I hate to disappoint you Teresa, you are not going to be able to keep this bear after all."

Teresa asked her why not? My daughter said, "Well, Margaret was my mother's name, and pearls were her favorite."

Fast forward many years, and now that I have had my picture taken and it is on Teresa's website, her photographer, Ric Matkowski, Owner of Images by Ric, chose me to highlight by making sure I looked my absolute best for all of you to see!

There are not words to express to show how excited I am that I get to be a part of Teresa's story and that my daughter fell in love with me.

YOLANDE

Hi. My name is Yolande. I came into Teresa's life in an unusual way. I had to track her down and reach out to her through her brother. My daughter was looking for Teresa, and while it took a while to find her, find her, she did. She really didn't have far to look; my sister was a neighbor to a good friend of hers. She also has a friend who is a cousin to one of my daughter's husband's. It is a small, small world after all.

Teresa met with all my three children at one of my daughter's homes. They had a lovely chat one evening. My children were on the fence, as to whether or not they should turn my much-loved, fur coat into teddy bears.

They just couldn't decide. Teresa was so patient with them.

My children just wanted to honor me and acknowledge how important my fur coat was to me. Without them saying so, the look they had between each of them was... *Well, I'm not sure, what do you think? Should we? Shouldn't we?*

Little did they know then...

Finally, they made the decision to proceed with three teddy bears. One for each of my two daughters, and one for my son.

They decided on what size, whether I should be boys or girls, what could be done with the lovely lining in my coat, should they put my initials on the bears' paw pads...so many questions....so many decisions...

The meeting finally came to end, and Teresa was about to take my lovely coat with her. At the door, she paused and said "You know, we should check your Mom's pockets to make sure there isn't anything there that you need to keep. You never know what's inside pockets."

Oh, what surprises awaited them!

Right there before them, out from my pocket came an article I had saved, from a newspaper long ago. It said, "...turn your fur coats into teddy bears."

Oh, and I had also found a poem for them to make certain they knew I wanted teddy bears made for them .... It goes like this...

> *Here's a very special teddy bear*
> *Made from my very favorite coat*
> *Hold it, love it, and hug it tight*
> *And it will be there day and night.*
> *It can't replace the love that I held dear*
> *But it's a reminder that my love is there*
> *So, when you're sad and feeling blue*
> *Hug your bear as though I hugged you.*
> -Unknown

Their mouths dropped open and they all looked at each other and said, "Yes, Mom wanted us to make teddy bears from her fur coat, let's proceed."

Teresa put this poem as a "tag" on the bottom of my bum for each of the bears as a reminder that yes, I loved them all dearly, please remember me.

While Teresa has shared only a few of her "bear stories" with you, it is important for you to know and understand, that her bears come alive and speak to her when she adds their ears and eyes and any other finishing touches.

Each bear is unique and special.

She utilizes as much of the fur coats as possible and is careful not to waste or discard unnecessarily.

We, bears on our own, aren't what it is all about. It is always about what we represent, the special memories we hold, and how we make you feel.

It's about creating a legacy for you to remember that special person in your life.

It is a reminder.

They never really leave you.

ABOUT DEBORA HOLLICK

Debora J. Hollick, *The Smash Through Mentor*, is an International Speaker, 3x International #1 Best Selling Author, Intuitive Consultant & Strategist, Trainer, and Coach.

She helps businesses and professionals ★ smash confusion, ★ solve chaos, and ★ stop cussing, while they are resolve challenges. Her clients say, *"It feels like, receiving a warm, energy hug, while also receiving a gentle kick in the pants!"*

Debora speaks on many topics, a few of which are:

- A Selfie Of A Different Sort,
- Listen To The Whispers Or...Get The 2x4! And
- Do You Have A Bully Living Within?

She is the author of *Live Life In W.O.W! Nuggets of Wonder~Openness~Wisdom* anthology book, Companion Playbook, and founder of the **W.O.W! Concept** events,~ planned to launch during 2023.

Contact Debora:
https://www.linkedin.com/in/deborajhollick/
https://www.facebook.com/groups/604879661411370
https://www.facebook.com/SmashThroughMentor/
Debora@smashthroughmentor.com

Made in United States
Orlando, FL
16 December 2022

26704481R10111